AF345300

The Dawn in Britain, Volume 5

THE DAWN IN BRITAIN

The Dawn in Britain

BY CHARLES M. DOUGHTY

AUTHOR OF

'TRAVELS IN ARABIA DESERTA'

VOLUME V

LONDON: DUCKWORTH & CO.

3 HENRIETTA STREET, COVENT GARDEN

1906

Edinburgh: T. and A. Constable, Printers to His Majesty

Genio

Terrae Britannicae [1]

[1] *Corpus Inscr. Lat.* 1113.

BOOK XVII

5—A

ARGUMENT

THOROLF and Antethrigus march together, to recover royal Verulam. Battle before the town; which is taken, and the Roman garrison therein slain. Higelac.

Camulodunum beleaguered; queen Embla sends forth all women and impotent folk. Roman navy enters the river's mouth. Caratacus languishing to death, is, by Embla, saved forth, in a covered cart. Guitelnus, the city's magistrate, bids all, which would have saved their lives, go forth. On the morrow, hurt and aged Britons, and few warriors, which remain with him, and druids, burn themselves, in the temple-court of Camulus!

Claudius, at afternoon, drawn of elephants, in the royal chariot of Cunobelin; enters the dune gates. Asiaticus, a noble Roman, bids to banquet, the emperor Claudius. They sup together. On the morrow, Cæsar lustrates his navy; and the legions. He makes donation, to his soldiers; and bestows military ornaments. Claudius decrees, that here were founded a Colony of Roman soldiers. He bestows the diadem, on the treacherous Cæsarian Briton kings, Bericos and Cogidubnos. Asiaticus sets forth stage-plays, before the army and Claudius. Captive Britons are sold, under the spear.

Claudius, hasting to his triumph, embarks for the Continent. He comes, in Gaul, to Lugdunum, city of his nativity. That town's folk decree public honours, to their fellow citizen, imperial Claudius. Herod Antipas is in exile, there. Come again to Rome, Claudius sets forth a great triumph-spectacle of his Britannic war.

In Britain, Troynovant submits. Vespasian subdues Vectis. Moridunion is taken. Vespasian's legion winters at the Baths-of-Sul.[1] Story of the king Bladud. Aged Dumnoveros, fighting with the Romans, is slain. Durovernium taken, Kentish havens submit then, to the Roman arms. The saints and brethren succour the poor, in Avalon.

[1] Now Bath.

THE DAWN IN BRITAIN

BOOK XVII

WAS in that fatal sun, when the blue tribes
Were smitten, under walls of Camulodunum ;
That the ethling Thorolf, with stout bands of
  Almains,
And wains, marched forth, from merchant Troyno-
  vant.
His noble heart is set, reconquer Verulam,
That royal dune, whilom of sire Cunobelin :
Whereof might tiding spring, to Wittig's ears.
But lords which should, with him, Marunus, Golam,
Have marched, to win again Cunobelin's town ;
Crowned with oakleaves, and leading blue caterfs ;
Valorous contend, to-day, with Roman legions ;
Before great Trinobantine dune, by Colne :
Where, déstiny is, they both, to-night, must lie,
Out, in cold mead, among the battle-slain.
Nathless, shall Cadern's generous son, Marunus,

3

THE DAWN IN BRITAIN

(Though occupy his limbs a mortal frost,)
Not breathe forth, in that field, his warlike ghost.
  Now, in place called the Three Wents ; where
    Verulam path
Verges, by heath, beyond the Potter's Wood ;
Behold, where long-haired bands already pass !
Are they blue Britons, East-men ; and them leads
He, whom late Aulus vanquished, Antethrigus :
Unto whom appearing Andates, to-night,
Hath promised Victory, before Verulamion !
Whence, at new day, three thousand valiant warriors,
(And, most-part, those were clients of his house,
Which   gathered,   to   their   lord,   erewhile,   in
    forest ;)
Exulting in this hope, with him, march forth.
  Known, from afar, each other ; then approach
Almains and Britons, with loud welcome shouts !
Soon Antethrigus, who stands, in shrill scythe-cart ;
And Thorolf, ethling, sitting on white horse,
Knit warlike hands : so march they on, one host.
  Ere noon, strange portent ! in Caer Verulam walls,
Romans hear, from the trembling element,
Sound confuse trump, shout, din of divine arms.
Woden and Thunor, furious gods of Almains,
Inspiring in their breasts, make ethlings' harness

Seem light on their proud chests; their weapons
    reeds,
Which, of themselves, seem wag in their tough
    hands:
Force they, to Almains' limbs, impart of steeds.
Then riseth, in them, as a tide divine,
Diffused in all their veins. To victory, intend
Their hearts ; or else to sup, this night, with Woden !
Contend Icenians, with them, in swift course ;
In whom, the battle-rage, breathes Camulus.

    Half-afternoon was, when, lo, Verulam walls !
Rome's watchmen, on that guard-hill of the dune ;
And who on tower-gate stand of Cassiobellan,
Sun-glittering host descry, and hostile arms.

    Straight Ulpius, tribune, bids his clarions sound.
Cohorts assemble, in the market-place.
He, Roman, and disdaining, pent in walls,
To suffer barbare siege, leads forth his cohorts ;
And them erects, in threefold battle ordinance.

    Britons, in thick caterfs, ascend and Almains !
Who, wading Ver, had seemed, now, dreadful wood,
Of wavering spears, to little-statured soldiers.
Their dukes, with shout, lead on : they fall on
    Romans,
With immane brunt, above the human wont.

THE DAWN IN BRITAIN

As fierce ureox, that pusheth with his horns,
The Icenian hero fares.   All, in his wrath,
He brings, to naught, that stands before his face !
And when brake Calad, in his hand, his glaive ;
Resistless giant, he with outrageous lance,
Among them wades.   At each stroke, he some
    Roman
Strews ; piercing, (through hard shield or brazen
    plate,)
With fury, his body, or his open gorge.
So spurns, (that came this land, to reave, of Brennus,
In long row-ships,) their dying carcases !
The furrows run, with strange Italic blood :
For smitten was this battle, in eared field.
    Thorolf, like mower, reaps Rome's sharded ranks.
Him follows main of warriors, from the Elbe,
Terrible of countenance, of unvanquished gods.
In the ethling's hand, is Brennus' divine blade ;
Which sledged, (men say,) for Balder, the bright-
    faced,
Brown dwarves : it heired, of blessed gods, his
    house.
And Romans fall, like reeds, before his force.
That battle-king, above the mortal press,
Surges great shouldered stature, in bright harness.

Seems Thorolf's helm to lighten!   Sacred boar,
(Gold-bristles,) is, of gold, the hero's crest.
(Token of Nertha, Elbe-land's mother-goddess.)
And, lo, amidst the fray, down-lighted raven,
On Thorolf's neck, sent from his father Woden !
Which, with his wings, doth fan the ethling's heat.
Whence yet more grows his pulse, that seems his brand
Thor's[1] hammer, which thwart-smites dark rumbling
    clouds.
He went through Romans, as they were a mist.
    Not otherwise than as some nesting thrush,
In sweet spring time, her gaping birds to feed,
Hacks silly snails, till she the mangled life
Out-snatch ; his hard unconquerable force,
Shields bursts, shares sharded plate, on Romans'
    breasts ;
And drives the groaning spirits from their pasht chests.
Than these, none mightier lords have fought in
    Britain !

Erewhile, save that wherein fights Antethrigus,
In field, was seen no scythe-cart.   From thick grove,
War-wheels then issue, of an antique guise ;
Whereon stand two old warriors, whose hoar locks

----

[1] The same as Thunor or Thunder.

Fly backward, in the wind!   Loud, on war-gods,
Those call ; in that, with furious team, they set
On, slay, pursue, outlandish enemies.
For Scævola seen to fall, noblest in Verulam,
Of Roman knights, his soldiers turn their backs.

And were those certain brethren, Pen and Keth,
Champions, whilere, in king Cunobelin's court.
Stout Keth, (who foster-sire to Togodumnos,)
Hurler from chariot was of the king's spears :
But Pen was tamer of the royal steeds.

Bereaved of sons, those sally, anew, to wars.
Howbe, with eld, now stiffened are their joints ;
And pith lack their old limbs.   The sires' intent,
On whom, to-day, new battle-woodness falls ;
Is smiting them, before whom fell their sons,
(Camog and Morfran,) end with the self death.

Last, when forsaken of all, Silvanus Ulpius
Had turned his face, and spurs set to his horse ;
Him, lightly, hart-swift Thorolf overran,
Upon his feet : and from tall steed, that tribune,
Smote, with gore-dropping plat of Brennus' blade,
Bruising his helméd brain, adown alive.

Thorolf, left Ulpius swooning, on the grass ;
Commands his thanes, him spoil of arms and
    bind!

His oath, to accomplish, he o'erseas had sworn ;
To slay some Roman captain on hill-tomb,
By Thames, in Bret-land, of the hero Brennus !
(Glories great Thorolf, to be called his son.)
He, loud, invoking then, his sires' sire Woden ;
After Rome's flying cohorts follows fast ;
To strew them, with his spear, kill and cut-off.
But envying, whilst thus Romans fall, some god,
The glory of Thorolf ; Ulpius, not yet bound,
Come to himself, and now despaired of health ;
With his own secret steel, did smite himself,
Even as his mother's uncle, Uticensis ![1]
And sighed, in that he breathed his spirit forth ;
In him, should none unworthy bands, distain
The honour of his ancient noble house !
So dies, not vanquished, midst his enemies.
Britons, which lately thralls, shut in their dune,
Seen these things, from the walls, rise, and slay
    Romans.
They all within put to avenging sword,
Man, wife and child, that bear a name of Rome :
Then run they, all bloody ; and cast up Verulam
    gates !
Where now, o'er Roman dead, in, boisterous, pass

[1] The minor Cato.

THE DAWN IN BRITAIN

Almains, Icenians.   Thorolf enters first :
Great glory is his, win Britain's royal dune !

   Were Pen and Keth remained, in cart, without ;
With Antethrigus, who yet courseth Romans :
Nor, in Caer Verulam, enter will that duke ;
For vow he made, he would not lodge in walls ;
Nor wash his face, nor comb his ravelled locks ;
Till driven, from Britain, were again Rome's legions ;
And should they have the narrow seas, repassed.
   Then brother spake to brother ; and the spears,
(Which, in their stout old hands, have fugitive
      Romans,
Till evening, slain,) both cast, from cart, to ground :
Why linger we?   See'st not, my father's
      son;
How goeth low, to her setting, this late sun?
When, windows closed in heaven, should
      overflit,
Under steep skies, our souls, this field, all
      night;
Nor find, with happy spirits, a resting
      place.
Their team they stayed: then lighted both to ground ;
And each fell, groaning, on his weapon's point !

THE DAWN IN BRITAIN

And sink their corses, at the powdered wheels,
Of their scythe-cart, and hooves of their war-steeds.
  Which seen, come running Britons, from the dune.
They lift those old proud warriors dead, in wain :
So lead towards Verulam gates, or were they cold.
And whilst give gods yet twilight on the ground ;
Thereunder they them hastily grave ; as druids
Read and appoint.   And many, in dream, to-night
Met Pen and Keth : whose praises bards shall chant !

  Britons, to Andates, heap, in Verulam streets,
All spoils of Romans.   Washed, from battle-blood,
His hands and war-weed, wends, to sup, now Thorolr,
In king Cunobelin's court, with earls of Almains.
  But so it grieved his high heart, to behold,
What scathe, in royal dune, was wrought, of Romans ;
He would not enter, in king's wasted hall ;
Where, with his Briton kinsmen, Togodumnos
And Caradoc, warlords both, he lately supped
The dulcet mead, in antique cups of gold.
Nor, after meat, yet sitting at high board,
Would the ethling drink, though Roman wine be
      brought,
Sap of a tree which drink, men say, their gods !
He it disdains ; nor Bragi's bowl he tastes :

THE DAWN IN BRITAIN

Nor Thorolf hearkens to victorious lays ;
Though Higelac be come in, his father's reeve ;
Who newly arrived, with three swift keels, from Elbe ;
And song-smith, passing-well, in Almains' tongue,
Can make and chant, of heroes and high gods ;
But weary of fight and darkened is his mood !
Of Higelac fabled is, in forest Almaigne ;
How light-elves, of the stream, (whose shining weed
Of glass,) him, elf-born, out of faery, brought ;
And cradled left, by moonlight, in the house,
For his own child, of Leofstan, the king's steward ;
Where was he fostered then, of woman's breast !
But grown the babe, (and being now of man's
    right ;)
One morn, before the sun, twixt sleep and wake,
In Easter-month,[1] when gin sweet birds to sing ;
Lying, by shield and arms, in his king's hall ;
Midst Wittig's slumbering warriors ; Oin, elf-king,
Horn, (heirloom old, hight Gold-beak, mongst home-
    sprites,)
Him brought, of Woden's dearworth stolen mead ;
Whereof his young lips tasting, he received
Shape-craft,[2] as fiery billows in his breast !

[1] The Teutonic April; named from (A. Sax.) *Eostra,* goddess.
[2] A. Sax. *scopcræft* ; (*poesis,*) the Poets' art.

THE DAWN IN BRITAIN

Was he ; sith steersman bold, and royal steward,
Who that lay made, wide-known yet in North parts,
Hight Wisdom of the gods. Him in Elbe's
    forest,
Men say, had, (his first Summer's sea-fare past,)
Taught antique spirits, of the white water-floods ;
That stream from hills of heaven. Wont rise, at
    even,
Those singing clear, to harps of golden sound,
Under the hollow wave of waterfalls !

  Cold fleeting Ver, mingled with blood, ran
    down,
All night ; and corses of slain steeds and men,
Cumber his sedgy brinks. From Camulodunum,
Vast field of swollen Britons' carcases ;
Foul ravens flit, to sup at Verulam,
Of fallen Romans. Few, 'scaped forth, have
    round
Them, in that twilight, mounded bank of mould ;
Weak fence, in an hill-place. Wounded the most,
In the dank herb, they lie, and daze their hearts !
  When risen new cheerful light is, on wide earth,
Those Roman soldiers, creeping faintly forth,
Did leaves, for hunger, gnaw, of trees and grass.

Then footsteps finding, of some fore-past cohorts ;
They journey on, fearful ; staying, who are hurt,
On wild staves of lopt boughs. Dread fills their
    hearts ;
(Had many, in flight, their shields and harness cast ;)
Whiles they pass forth, in hostile wilderness,
By unknown paths ! where hips and bramble-berries,
And worts, those, in the way, must seek for meat.

    For naught those, (minding overthrow of Varus,[1]
In stories old,) now cure ; might they but save
Their weary lives ! When of those fugitives,
The first, to Colne brinks, now sixth eve, arrive,
Already, is their discomfiture known to Aulus.

    Lighted one Tertius, servant to the quæstor,
(His *tabellarius*, mongst the Gaulish horse ;)
One, whom had raging spear of Antethrigus
Hurt. Weary after battle ; he, with few,
Which, scaped to horse, had all that night ridden
    forth,
Towards rising stars. He lights, by the brook
    Maran ;
To rest, and wash his angry wound and bind.
But feeling come, with trembling, the cold death ;
Rent Tertius, hastily, roll of his account :

[1] Vol. iv. p. 26.

THE DAWN IN BRITAIN

And part, (on Jovis Vindex, calling !) binds
He, round light scabbard of his horseman's glaive ;
And wrote, *Ex clade Romanorum*, VER.
So cast, in Maran's stream, his dying hand !
   Certain, next eve, post-riders to Longport
(With Belges, guides,) it fleeting found, by hap,
In ford of Lea ; where watered they their steeds.
Those one sent back then, who this bare to Aulus.
Have perished, all which lingered in the path,
Fainting with wounds and thirst and weariness ;
Whom finding, angry Icenians did cut-off.

   Lo, Roman towers, that now wide walls o'erlook
Of Trinobantine war-god Camulus.
Is sway in some and battery of ram-head beams :
From other, mighty archery, of steel-stringed engines;
Launching both great winged darts, as shafts, and
     stones
Of poise : walls, whereon now beleaguered Britons,
May stand uneath. Few days, they, yet, them fence,
With countermures, gainst that strong siege of
     Romans.
   Helm-clad, like Belisama, lo, queen Embla,
With archers' guard and spears, walks hourly round :
And where, war-lady, Embla stedfast mounts,

THE DAWN IN BRITAIN

There power, with beauty and grace seems of a
    goddess.
And who is there, hearing her heavenly voice,
His shield not strains, in sterner wise, and arms.
Who, even the aged, feels not then revive,
(Beholding her, clear glory of womankind !)
The flowers of spring-time, in his withered blood ?
All, after Embla look, where she doth pace.
    And weight is aye, of sorrowful dark thought,
And travail, in all breasts, for Caradoc,
And cannot be repressed ; because not yet,
He, Shield-of-Britons, wakes out of his trance ;
(Fighting, for mastery, in his royal veins,
The radical heat, with venim's deadly force.)
    Murmur, who barefoot go before that porch,
(Where the lord lieth, not tasting meat, save oft
Is little milk and mead poured, twixt his teeth,)
That Togodumnos perished by a shaft.
Opinion also, mongst blue Britons, is ;
(It druids sought out, of some Numidian captive ;
Which this, by signs, to them, declared !) the shot
Was tinct in venim ; (namely of hornéd asp,
Bush-adder of their droughty wilderness ;)
Whence must the strongest die ; whom not pre-
    serve,

THE DAWN IN BRITAIN

The gods ! By day and night-time wakes queen
    Embla,
Singing aye spells, by loved Caratacus.

   Archers of Andred, nigh five hundred bows,
Keep Camulus' walls ; else weak were their defence,
Which hold the dune, wives, striplings, and old
    men.
Each eve, they watch, to dawn ; come day, till even,
For the returning armies of blue Britons.
   When that first rampire, which girds-in their town,
Have Romans won, part-razed, and choked the
    dyke;
(Wherein sharp tree-trunks, which so bound, beneath ;
And wreathed their boughs, and that in rows, above ;
They, by the soldiers, could not be removed ;)
The inner bank, their miners under-delve ;
Bank of heaped earth, it is ; that, Gaulish wise,
Bonded with pillared beams, and rammed with stones ;
Gainst which prevail, not lightly, battery of engines.
Moreo'er, by day and night-time, have relays,
Of cohorts, digged wide trenches, in the plain ;
To lead away the currents of the Colne,
That naught might, to the sieged, but brine, remain ;
Which daily infloweth, twice, of the salt tide.

Wherefore, when whelmed is now, on the low
    world,
Night's hollow shadow, without gleam of stars ;
The queen, all who unapt, by kind or age ;
(Wives, little ones, old wights,) to fight on walls,
Gathered about her, in the market-place ;
Sends weeping forth, with three-score Andred bows ;
Where path, o'er fenny strand, lies, at low ebb :
And thence, by privy ford, unwatcht of Romans,
(Through favour of some god,) those silent wade.
Seemed Camulus go before them, in a cloud ;
That, unmarked, they pass sentinels ; and beyond,
Come safely o'er Colne fen, soon those take wood !
    Is Cartismandua sitting, sad in bower !
She, though the dune be shut in, by assiege ;
And Caradoc lies at point of death, she hear,
Comes no more forth ; she wakes, by Vellocatus.
Though wood her heart be, for her squadrons lost ;
Would not she reck of loss, would but crude heavens
Her, ah ! restore this deadly Vellocatus !
Whose wan lips seems already, to have kissed,
Goddess, abhorred, of death ! would but her save,
Her gods, from this last loss of hoped-for love !
    On Morrigu, she, great queen of witches all,
Loud frantic calls ; and on false Arianrod,

THE DAWN IN BRITAIN

For succour, goddess of the silver wheel.
By spells, sith, summoned her familiar spirits ;
She enquires, how fatal stars, might from their
     courses,
Be wrested, and compelled the very gods ?

     Again, the Roman siege, till eve, endures.
Then carracks' sails and masts, of long-beaked ships
Seen standing, navy of Rome, into Colne-mouth !
Had tarried them the wind, which veered, when past
They were Thames' frith ; and fell on them, sea-reek :
Whence the third morrow, (being Southward cast ;)
Returned, by the two Forelands, steering North ;
They, fetched Thames' tiding mouth, had safely
     passed ;
And Fowlness sith, ingathering with the land ;
Where seemed them, the element snowed of feathered
     kinds ;
Whose clangor like to voice, at dawn, of legions,
That levy camps.   Night-time, by stormy banks;
Where hollow waves and mingled Syrtes seemed
Contend, and yelling Britons from sea-brinks ;
They slowly sailed.   But undescried Rome's navy
Was, of those swart, wing-breasted, long-ribbed, keels,
With nimble dragon-stems ; which for them wait,

THE DAWN IN BRITAIN

Under the grey East wind, of Saxon pirates.
Land-inward now they fleet on Colne's salt tide.

 Sent Embla ; and called then elders of the dune.
And come those, soon, in king's hall, to the queen ;
They do behold, (who seems, ah, nigh to death !)
Laid on a bed, warsire Caratacus.

 And seeing now they, by sea and land, beset,
Not longer, might endure ; but every hour,
This city in danger lies of leaguering Romans :
She deems, (as was established before-hand,)
The sire to save forth, in a covered cart.

 In troublous hour, of sorrowful last loss,
They thank queen Embla, and praise her pious read.
Make ready, a light wain soon, some, and yoke-
  steeds ;
Other call Andred archers, for their guard,
From the sieged walls. Who noblest do therein,
Lo, reverent lift, (on pillows, now borne forth,
Swooning, yet all his sense dismayed,) sire Caradoc !

 With mournful cheer, and harnessed as she is,
Queen Embla mounts. His sacred head upbear
Her wifely knees : and troubled cast to ground,
Britons their weary looks ; when now they fare.
For, (queen of all their hearts !) were, without her,
As moonless night, this dune besieged, on Colne.

She, more than walls, was rampire of the town.
They, lifting up sad eyes, on Caradoc, gaze,
Britain's warsire, whom should they see no more ;
Looking, for their own deaths, upon the morrow !
　Now covertly, on float of beams, is wafted o'er,
The king's wain ; to yond fenny brinks of Colne.
(Claudius, new muster maketh of his legions ;
Wherefore his horse and cohorts were withdrawn,
By favour of the gods, down in the plain,
To hindward of the dune, this afternoon !)
Three hundred Andred bows, the warlord ward :
And as they from salt strand, up, fearful fare ;
Much Embla, in heart, prays, to her Briton gods,
They might win safe, to far-off fords, of Ouse !
　Queen Cartismandua, sith, (to whom queen Embla
Had message sent ;) from Camulus' river-walls,
Now dusking the air, in like sort, lo, outfares :
The Northern queen outfares, with Vellocatus !
That prince upholding, in Brigantine chariot,
Drawn of white steeds.　And leans his manly face,
That languishing seemeth dead, on the queen's breast !
Whence, falling long adown, his golden locks,
Are hers, in lovely wise, confused with his.
Brigantine guard, (tall champions of her house,)
March, with the queen's wain forth, as sixty spears.

But, sith, she her steals from Embla, in dim
    night;
When passing forest-places; and is cause
The cold chaste looks, to Cartismandua, are loath,
Of that sad queen, still seeming her reprove.

  In this long glooming, come, like dim pine-
    grove,
Those Roman masts and yards: that anchors shoot,
Where Colne's fleet[1] spreads, below the dune; and
    deep
Thence, slides the stream. Then mariners, in their
    ships,
Then soldiers, thrice, loud shout, in Latin tongue!
Their cry passed the hill-dune : it heard the legions,
Whose double voice makes answer, from two *val-*
    *lum*s !
  Quoth doting Claudius ; that now, after meat,
Sits in the imperial tent, with purpled captains,
Par-breaking, nodding his cup-shotten face ;
Our ships, *Meherc'les!* drink-mates, fel-
    low-soldiers,
From Tenedos be come in; whose wooden
    wombs,

---

[1] A. Sax. *fleót*, estuary.

THE DAWN IN BRITAIN

Shall bring, to-night, forth harnessed Roman
    soldiers ;
And Britain's high-walled Ilium, shall burn !
  To Colne-side, hath sent Aulus, Roman knights,
With Gaulish horse ; in Cæsar's name, commanding
The præfect, Cælius, he disbark his soldiers :
And early, at morrow, when should they hear trumpet,
Beyond dune walls, of there assailing cohorts ;
They mount up likewise from their river *vallum*.
  Shipmen, which climbed now their main-tops, surview
That town, in part, of the blue barbare Britons !
Behold, how, in a twilight market-place,
Go thronging people armed ; mongst whom, white druids.

  Those sit, in council, in the temple-court ;
Where warriors come in, from round-leaguered walls ;
Other are hurt, are some old impotent wights.
Guitelnus, reverend, white-browed magistrate,
Speaks, mongst that dying people of Camulus,
Whilst all give ear ; hark speaks, with submiss voice ;
Over the river quagmires, lies yet path,
Where the sea-lavender and salt samphires
    grow :
Haste them, whoso would saved their lives,
    there pass !

THE DAWN IN BRITAIN

A weeping company, lo, for their homes lost,
Bearing, their stuff, in sacks, with fearful foot,
Outwend !   They Colne, in the cold glooming, wade.
Camulus, the most, of those, then saved : but met,
With other, men in barks, (armed waterers,
Of the fleet-soldiers ;) that few having slain,
Of those poor Britons ; bind, for thralls, the rest.
　　Guitelnus caused, be delved, this night, deep pit
And also wide, under their market-place :
Where thing, which cannot be, by fire, consumed,
Might buried lie.   This done, he, magistrate,
Cast public wealth in ; druids cast temple-gifts ;
Cast private men their good !   Trampled of feet,
Last rammed they, even with the ground, the place :
That when were taken the dune, might stranger Romans
　　Romans
Not find to spoil this substance of poor Britons !

　　That remnant, lo, in their wide sieged-round walls,
(Which may, no more, a golden sun, behold,
In heaven,) sit armed, round house of Camulus.   Much
Those commune, sad, in sheen moonlight ; and watch,
Their devout eyes, that starry pomp, on high ;
Wherein be mansions of their fathers' gods !
Beseeching those, remember Foster Britain,

After their deaths !   Guitelnus spake of wars,
Of Tasciovant,[1] and divine Eppilos,[2]
In ancient days.   Vain thing, quoth he, it were,
Old unweld wight, that may not handle, more,
His weapon, seek save, by unseemly flight,
Few days, (days void of honour,) of vile life.
 His wise lips ceased to speak ; for, even now, springs
Ambrosial sacred dawn, of the light-god.
And hearken, a far-off bray, ah, heavy note,
If any feared to die, of Roman clarion !
 Hark !   Britons' watchmen cry, that come the legions !
All death-vowed, with Guitelnus, then uprose.
Their druids them lead, in Camulus' sacred court,
With solemn tread, his temple-house, thrice round.
Then, seeing, of all their deaths, the looked-for moment
Arrived is ; puts hand, lo, Guitelnus, erst,
To eaves of the god's porch ; and pluckt-down thatch !
The like do all : then, passed forth, in the street,
Men rent down spar and rafter.   They sith heap
These round about them, in their temple-place.

---

[1] Father of Cunobelin.   [2] (Or Eppillos ;) a son of Commius.

THE DAWN IN BRITAIN

Utters already, in heaven's Eastern steep,
Born of vast night, new day, his teeming head !
Guitelnus stretched, towards that eternal god,
Amongst his citizens his two palms; loud prays,
Abate, lord, the flames' torment, and abridge
This fleshes anguish; ease our dying smart!
Be as a glaive, of hero's hand, pluckt forth,
From scabbard, the swift passing of our
    spirits ;
And be exalted to the deathless gods!
Kindred and friends, holding each-other's hands,
Embrace, for the last time, and kiss. Loud
    druids,
Intone, in this extremity, antique hymns ;
Of virtue, against the eager edgéd pangs,
Of raging element, that shall on them seize !
Priests, from the altar, bear forth flaming brands !
All stedfast take : they fire then halm and wood !
With furious high intent, those Britons' throats,
Shout, (from amidst their burning,) saviour gods !
Who fall down scorched, soon smother, in thick
    smoke :
Thus all those perish, with a constant heart !
Dread, hungry-tongued, wild nimble-footed flame,
Roars of their torment. Soon the wattle-streets,

THE DAWN IN BRITAIN

It raught.   Of hill-set, leaguered, Camulodunum,
Surges vast balefire! on the morning wind,
With flakes of flame upblown, stench, falling ash.
   Legions,   in   march,   behold,   amazed!   Cries
      Claudius,
Long, gazing-on; Ha, Ilium doth burn!
Sound out the legate's clarions, that halt legions:
Then cease fleet-soldiers from their river part!
   Noon was, when Cæsar sent forth certain knights,
With Gaulish horse.   Passed undefenced dune gates,
Those circumspectly enter; and burned streets,
Behold; all cindered, full of smouldering heaps!
Wherein those spoils, long promised, lie consumed;
Which should have eased, and even enriched Rome's
      legions.

   The next hour, lo, in sight of all, draw in
Gigantic yoke of Afric elephants,
The *imperator* Drusus Nero Claudius;
In chariot standing, of Caratacus,
For the more glory.   And was that winged white
      war-cart
Taken in the battle.   Kowain and Venutios,
Leapt, when o'er-yerked Goldhoof the beam, to
      grass,

Down, hastily ; and they with sharp skeans shared his
    trace.
Constrained to leave, midst mortal press, king's
    chariot ;
Those saved the royal team, and that uneath !
Themselves scaped hardly away, on the steeds' backs.
    Cæsar commands, when Camulus' gate he passed,
To raise, in *forum* burned, of Britain's Ilium ;
(Which vapours yet, like a vast dying pyre,
Full of white bones of Britons,) the imperial
Pavilion.   Of the bitter reek, recks Claudius
But small ; nor stench even of his enemies'
    corses !
    Lo, in the prætorian *tabernaculum*, erst,
He sitting, of his legate ; bravely endites
And seals now imperial letters, to Vitellius,
His colleague, (namely in that year's consulship :)
Sith, to Rome's Senate, writes magnific tidings ;
Under his auspices, how Britannia prostrate,
Lies ; their *metropolis* burned : blue Britons tamed ;
He added hath, another world, to Rome.

Now Asiaticus, who, from Gaul, outsailed ;
To wait, in Britain, on the imperial state ;
Being Epicure's own son, and friend to Claudius :

(By certain his procurers, in Gauls' camps,
Men which can speech of Britons,) daily enquires ;
What dainty pleasures Britain doth afford ?
Yet lately showed this senator, in the field,
Was sprung, of worthy loins, his noble blood ;
That could he, (as could Luculle,) both fight and eat.
In thickest strife, named tribune of a legion,
(For Dolabella hurt !) he led his soldiers,
All   day ;   and   with   what   countenance   wont   are
        Romans,
To lean, with flower-crowned brows, at solemn feasts.
   This   lord,   to   banquet   bids   now   the   emperor
        Claudius ;
Of such poor wilding thing, to taste, to-night,
As, (this side seas,) have found his Gaulish servants ;
Of any singular savour, delicate ;
Sturgeon and lamprey and eel, with poignant sauce ;
Roebuck, and swan's fat roast, and snipes in paste.
And Chian, and Falernian wine he hath ;
And mulse, of a ripe grape, from Roman Alban ;
And oysters, which his shipmen fished, where Colne
To salt sea-flood, outgoes ; more sapidous
Than   what   fat   shells,   are   culled   longs   Tyrrhene
        strand.
   Is only for them twain, this supper dight.

Shall maiden-captives serve them, which unlaced,
Unto the navel, loost-down their long locks ;
Of perfect feature, each esteemed a talent ;
And tickle the cold veins of Cæsar Claudius.
   Bright daughters of who noblest, mongst blue
      Britons,
(Were wont, companions of the Verulam's kings,
With them, on swift war-wheels, in field, to ride ;)
In what day taken was great Cunobelin's dune,
By sudden assault, wherein your brethren slain ;
Were ye also sold under Roman spear :
But not, for that, are bond your high-born hearts,
To your Land's insolent stranger enemies !
In your dear stedfast eyes, none wantonness
Hath dwelling-place : but their proud maiden-
      gaze,
Swart, little-statured Romans hath despised ;
Naught matchable, to your people's comely youth !
   Lo, the *triclinium*, in wide Seres tent,
(Without the walls, prepared, in a fresh mead,)
Of Asiaticus ! There, on purple, couched,
At board, now Cæsar Claudius, leaning, quoth,
Good is this loaf, of sheaf reaped by our
      soldiers !
We also some will fraught, in ship, to Rome.

Which grind shall Briton captives; and, thereof,
Be loaves set, on all tables, in Rome's streets;
What day, to Roma's citizens, we shall make,
(As erewhile *divus* Julius,) triumph-feast.
  Thy maidens, Friend, be like to marble nymphs,
Of Praxiteles, fetcht to Rome; those which
Stand in *impluvium* of our golden house;
Swift Cynthia's train, with silver bows; that seem,
And rattling quivers, on their budded breasts,
Leaping their high round flanks, on crystal feet,
Follow, with loud holloa! the chace in heaven.
  This, which beside me, my Valerius, hath
So bright long hair-locks, like ringed wiry gold,
And gracious breast, whereon sit wooing doves,
Meseems that famous Cnidian Aphrodite,

Great goddess mother of our Julian house;
Whereby   now   Thermæ   Agrippæ   are
        adorned.
What, damsel! mix me cup of Lesbian wine;
And give, with kiss of Venus' lips, of love.
Ha, these, that skill not of our Latin tongue,
Hold scorn of Cæsar, Asiaticus!
    And he; Have patience, lord; for they are
        barbarous!
Is the ignorant condition of all women,
They smally account of learning, wisdom,
        place;
But only of the first flower of a man's youth.
Would such not mock, and we their feet did
        kiss!
    This   Briton   loaf,   accords,   imperial
        Claudius,
Well with old Padan cheese of Mediolane,
And succory; and some mixt bitter herbs,
        therewith,
That make digestion sweet. A baxter, once,
That hurled the rumbling mill-stone, with
        his hand,
Robust, (hath left Terentius writ,) was Jove.
But more, and better, Epicurus saith;

Is earth Jove's mill-stone, whereon ever
    rolls,
(Frothing out infinite mortal miseries,)
His over-stone, grinding us men, to powder!
How cheers, to-night, my divine Claudius?
  And, ruckling, he; Methought, beyond the
    seas,
This isle another world. Valerius quoth,
And thou, our god, join'dst that new world,
    to Rome!
Old Bacchus, women vanquished, in the
    East;
And men him called a god, for there found
    wine:
But Claudius conquered world of giants and
    corn!
Though many were the gods of the blue
    Britons,
Prevailed our *divus* Claudius o'er them all.
  That men made gods, may sooner be
    believed,
Than gods men made. If gods this mortal
    mould
Shaped, what may deem men of their handi-
    work!

But that were children then the blesséd gods!
Not their craft's-masters. Were none list of
    meats,
And gracious Venus' mirth, and Bacchus'
    cups;
Who, longer than his nonage, would, therein,
Continue,   willingly!   Taste   victorious
    Claudius,
These shells, and shalt thou find them
    saporate,
Full of cold salty humour of the sea!
   And babbles Claudius, yexing in his talk;
Wherein lie pearls, which sought for Julius.
And he, to Britain, would invite Rome's Senate.
With vinegar, and tart wine of Tusculum,
They should esteem these oysters of the
    Colne!
   Thus Claudius spake, returning from his vomit;
With awry garland on his reeling pate,
Hemmed with white locks. Sith, for his stomach's
    health,
Of Britons' mead, (as Nestor's cup,) with leeks,
And certain powdered cheese, prepared, he drinks.
   Better than crabbéd wisdom of rough
    brows,

THE DAWN IN BRITAIN

Fond sophist's scorn, and sour wise-seem-
    ing looks;
(Being idle labour, of as vile account,
As daylong wafting of the forest's boughs,
Or quapping voice of the insensate waves,)
Is mirth, with present solace, and heart's
    feast.
  Thus Asiaticus : and cries, Her'kles! Claudius,
Thy saws sound better than Lucretius
    Carus;
Whose versets made 1 Attic in my youth;
When I the like, ha, my Valerius!
Or of more praise, could deftly turn, as
    this;
Celestial Sapience! Thou the phœnix bird,
That sings from heavenly spray, midst glit-
    tering stars;
Few are the days of men, in mortals' ears.
Are men the puppets of high heavenly gods.
Good reason then, were present joys em-
    brace;
And not some cold conceit of things that be
    not:
Fools they, that lead their lives, in wilful
    death.

THE DAWN IN BRITAIN

This from the drivelling lips of Cæsar Claudius ;
Who hardly, passed, three other years, in Rome,
Shall give, but only choice of unjust deaths,
To his companion Asiaticus !
As them, this so rich consular ere commanded,
Kindled have mariners of his ship, to-night,
(Without, in the poor Britons' cindered street,)
Watchfires of rosin, sandal, pleasant woods :
As in his gardens, on the Pincian hill,
(Magnific alleys, fountains, porches, arcs,
Adorned with many famous statues,
Of vanquished Hellas,) is his sumptuous wont ;
When any supped with him, of Cæsar's house.
And being now all made ready, newly invites
That noble Senator, imperial Claudius :
Who, yexing, walks forth, leaning on his hand ;
To gaze on Ilium, that yet flames, by night !

When Cæsar passed hath the pavilion's porch ;
Those damsels, suddenly, ah, greedy of their deaths !
Together, at a run, brast furious forth.
They, with their fisted hands, did smite aside
The watch : they beat back harnessed legionaries ;
Such pith, in women's arms, of the bold Britons !
The Almains' guard, then easily they forerun ;

THE DAWN IN BRITAIN

And, in yet smouldering pit, full of deep fires,
Where, of god Camulus, erst, an oracle was ;
Wherein now, fallen down, burning mighty beams !
Those noble virgins, frantic, start, alas !
Where fell they, in fiery powderous hearth, alas !
Brief was their torment ; surged a folding flame,
Crowns and consumes the glory of their gilt locks.
Their eyes, that wont, like molten stars, on Romans,
Shed scorn, be sightless cinders made, anon.
And veiled, in modest wise, round, that crude flame,
Their gracious limbs, that sink, down soon, in death.
Seemed, noble Briton maids, your saviour gods
Allay, of your pure flesh, the dying smart !
And yet they, a moment, wreathe, and did uprise ;
As when cast gobbets, on some temple-hearth !
Horrible, anon, arose, as smell of roast,
Of them, the parfume of whose life was such
As spring-time's virgin-bosom of the earth.
Then come few soldiers ; those gaze-in aghast !
And some was heard reproach old doting Claudius :
Yet answered other, Better thus their deaths,
Than, with long bondage, when deflowered
    their years ;
And slaves their maiden's honour had pos-
    sessed !

THE DAWN IN BRITAIN

So came, half-drunken, leaning on the hand
Of Asiaticus, fond imperial Claudius ;
Somewhat, by this new-rushing, in the night,
Amazed ; though follow guard of Ubba's spears.
Cæsar, at the pit's brink, stayed ; and admired,
To look on Priam's daughters' fiery grave !
Fell, from the blear eyes of his totty head,
Therein, few rheumy drops.   Might Scævola's
    deed,
In stories old, not be compared to this,
Quoth he, that burn themselves the Britons'
    dead!

When shines new sun, in heaven, with cheerful face ;
And lavrock mounts, from battle-bruiséd grass,
Of Colne ; and comes already crow, of cock,
To Claudius' ears, and clarions sound the watch :
He, from his surfeit, trembling wakes and pale.
  Sith, entered his chief captains ; their relation,
To the *imperator* made.   To Cæsar, Aulus
Records ; how had tumultuous sailed his army,
From Gaul.   Then he, grand *pontifex* of Rome,
Decrees lustrate, with old Etruscan rites,
His legions.   Cæsar, lo, and purpled dukes,
With vervain crowned, descend to Colne's green brinks.

THE DAWN IN BRITAIN

Erst priests, now noon, at altars, sacrifice,
Lo, hundred ewes and hundred farrow swine,
To Rome's trine greatest gods, and purge the navy.
Thereafter mounted Claudius, in his litter ;
Is, in large plain, borne forth.   With glittering
    ensigns,
At clarion's sound, now halt his warwont legions !
Lo, Cæsar seated, in imperial state,
On bank, made with degrees, of the green sods.
Conformable to old Rome's Etruscan rites,
(And whereof even a learned history hath
Claudius himself compiled,) should be led round
A swine, a ram, an ox ; with solemn pomp
Of priests and shrilling pipes ; and chief centurions,
His legate and who tribunes of the legions.
But certain Hellenes, flatterers, (libertines
Of his,) much labour to persuade fond Claudius ;
For his more dignity, by how much exceed
His deeds all memory of the former ages ;
That, in their stead, were led forth elephants.
Assented he ; and from his ivory throne,
Beckoning, sends for the huge slow-footed beasts :
(Howbeit he, for them, beves will sacrifice.)
Waver, the while, Rome's legions, glittering ranks,
As the sea's summer face : for soldiers' hearts,

Conscious of guilt, wax lean, in their proud breasts :
Misgives them, Claudius Cæsar cruel is,
More than Caligula.   Ís not also Claudius,
In Roman theatres, noted to be pleased,
To look on much blood-spilling, and men's deaths ?
What, and if Cæsar, that now is, commanded,
(Cast lots,) each tenth stand forth ; and punishment,
For their revolt, be, by their fellows' glaives,
Slain !   Yet they well have quit them, in the war ;
And Britain's fields have a large tithe consumed !
Standing on this, now on that other foot,
By turns, each, unto both opinions, leans.
    But their derne whisper, come to Cæsar's ears,
Through Sabine and chief tribunes of the legions,
Claudius that affects clemency of great Julius,
And magnanimity of divine Octavius,
Framing conformable countenance, to their, crowned
With laurel, sacred temple-images ;
He lightly passeth over their default,
According to the laws.   Consoles them, sith ;
Saying, they full wéll have borne them, in the
        war !
    Sith, *Victrix* names he, Conqueress of Britain,
His fourteenth legion ; which, in that sedition,
Had foremost been ; yet, since they passed Gaul's seas,

THE DAWN IN BRITAIN

In every field, most valorous those were seen.
He ordáins then, that be named the Saviour-legion,
Henceforth, those *pia* cohorts of Vespasian.
But Cæsar, on the ninth, Hispaniensis,
Displeased, laid, (legion, which their eagle lost,)
This punishment; that they hold still hindmost place,
Till ended were this war, in every march.
Soldiers then, knowing their lives saved ; in Britain,
Salute, (this second time,) *Imperator !* Claudius.

He, Cæsar, for have given him the gods,
So high felicity ; and his heart is glad,
(In token he would, there none were called to-day,
In question ; neither mourning be put on,
For any Roman, whom the laws have slain ;
In antique tablets writ, of frozen bronze ;)
Commanded, be his eagles crowned with bays,
And wreathed the bundles of his lictors' rods,
(Wands cut from Colne-Scamander's osier brinks,)
With flowers.   Moreo'er, donation to the army,
Sheep, without number, spoil of the poor Britons,
And thousand beves, he gives with wine of Gaul,
And double rate of corn, that might, to-night,
Make merry, in all their tents, victorious soldiers.

Sith, rising in his see, commemorates Claudius ;
Reading from scroll, what noblest deeds were done,

THE DAWN IN BRITAIN

Of Romans and allies, in Britain's war.
Hark Cæsar names them, fifteen legionaries,
Nor fewer of the warlike Gauls and Almains;
And loud, approach, commands them, one by one!
  They, before Claudius, on degrees of sods,
Lo, stand; that should, for valour, in the field,
Be crowned in all the army's open viewing.
Hath Cæsar certain baskets to his hand,
Prepared; wherein, be laid their glorious meeds,
Brooches and bracelets, golden collars, chains,
Phaleræ, and horsemen's silver ornaments.
  An oak-leaf-plight CROWN, by itself, is seen;
Guerdon, for life of citizen preserved!
  Loud spake then Cæsar; Fulve, of the ninth
    legion!
Receive, centurion, of thine *imperator*;
In testimony of thy military worth,
And good desert, this bracelet. Ever bear
It, on thy right arm, mongst thy fellow-
    soldiers!
And thou, Favoni Aper, knight of Rome,
Thine emperor, thee indues, with torque of
    gold.
Take this the glorious guerdon of thy merit,
And ever bear it, mongst thy fellow-soldiers!

THE DAWN IN BRITAIN

Unto thee, Novicius, of the second legion,
Decurion soldier, gives thine *imperator*,
This *hasta pura*, the exceeding meed,
Bear witness, all the army! of eagle saved!
It ever bear, amidst thy fellow-soldiers.
  So Claudius, to each one, praising their deeds;
The imperial words, rehearse then, to the legions,
Their captains with great voice; and sith their
        tribunes,
To men of the allies, both Gauls and Almains!
  Then, to his curule chair, of ivory, calls
Forth purpled Cæsar, lo, young Flavius Titus,
Beloved of all the army! and he, desirous,
And ruddy, ascends the imperial degrees,
Of the field-sods.   Reached forth the imperial hand :
Cæsar, him, for Corinium's conquered wall,
(Whereon stood erst Vespasian's manful son,
Stripling almost in years ; by whose proud deed,
That stronghold first, in hostile soil was won,)
Gives mural crown, behold, of the fine gold!
  Claudius himself, then, in his state, uprisen,
Before that valorous young man, knight of Rome!
(Soldiers' most coveted meed,) on him, the chapelet,
Whereon inscribed, *Ob Civem servatum !*
Imposed, for Roman citizen's life preserved.

For when the *pia* legion's duke, Vespasian,
Was fallen, from off his steed, mongst thronging
    enemies ;
He, many Britons having slain around,
Brought forth his father saved, on his own horse !
  From two-score thousand throats of legionaries,
Went up, so main voice, then, that, for the noise !
Birds fell to ground. And Cæsar sate, amazed ;
For common saw now is, in camps of soldiers,
That the three Fabii more have wrought than
    Aulus !
  Last, the emperor calls forth, some great-statured
    Almain ;
Whose name of barbare sound uneath might tongue
Of Claudius frame. This man saved Cnæus Geta ;
And when was broken the *framea*,[1] in his stiff hand,
He bet back Britons, with his only targe.
And he, with laud of the imperial mouth,
From Claudius, lo, receives broad golden brooch !
Joy, with much shouting, all the allies of Rome !
  Claudius absolves, sith, from their sacrament,
A thousand veteran soldiers ; and ordains,
(Thing which he dreamed of, three times, in the
    night,)

[1] The short lance of antique German warriors.

THE DAWN IN BRITAIN

Here founded were, a colony of veteran soldiers,
To be a rampart of Rome's laws and arms !
And officers he appoints thereto, and augurs ;
Of his *colônia*, like a camp of legions,
To mete out cross streets, *forum*-place and walls
Foursquare ; and measure thousand plots of glebe-
With stakes ; and beacons set up, through Colne
    fields.
And that be here coined money, he commands ;
Tribute, (as ere in Gallia,) of conquered nation.
    At morrow's day, the emperor puts his hand,
To compass in, with furrow, his new walls.
Lo, garlanded Claudius' sacred plough, with flowers !
Whose glittering share draw, yoked, instead of beves,
With slow foot forth, huge Afric elephants.

    The same day, have arrived Icenian legates,
Which of the traitorous part of Bericos.   Those,
Lo, crouched, at Cæsar's knees, do promise tribute !
But when is come in Bericos, from Longport ;
Binds Cæsar Claudius, sitting in his state,
His felonous brows, with royal diadem.
    Came the most Belges' kings, to Cæsar, there ;
(Disloyal ever to Cunobelin's house !)
And to imperial Rome, which rules the world,

THE DAWN IN BRITAIN

They do submit them, to live under tribute.
Confirms then Claudius, Regnian Cogidubnos,
O'er towns and tribes of Belges, to be king :
And purple giving and the diadem ;
Him names, in Britain, his imperial legate !
He attributes, also, to him, certain cohorts.
And Cæsar promised, to all Briton princes,
Which should submit them, pardon.   He remits
The public confiscation of their goods.

   Rose, clothed with purple weed, his temples crowned,
With gold-bright band, Cæsarian Cogidubnos !
And speaking, from the grees of Claudius' throne,
In Latin tongue, (he fugitive, learned in Roma ;)
He lifts to stars, the imperial benefits ;
And magnifies the high clemency of Claudius.
And, when here founded Cæsar's Roman town ;
He craves, that site were, midst the market-place,
Reserved ;   whereas, To CLEMENCY ; (namely of
    Claudius,)
Might temple, nations, grateful, of the Isle,
Build ; and be charactered on the gilded frieze,
BRITONS TO THE DIVINITY OF CLAUDIUS.

These things determined, from Britannia, Cæsar,
Hastes to his triumph, in imperial Rome.

THE DAWN IN BRITAIN

Rides, neath *Colonia* of Claudius, Roman navy ;
Now ready to heave anchor and hoise sail.
 The day before, to gratify the army,
And Claudius, emperor, Asiaticus ;
(Who now should journey forth, towards Rome, with
    Cæsar,)
In Camulus' meads, all at his proper cost,
Some little thing, a stage-play, would set forth.
Senec devised it, the philosophaster :
Yet somewhat, joining Asiaticus,
Thereto, of his own hand, had made his own ;
As who would vaunt him also gentle poet.
 Sit down, enranged, then, as in theatre ;
In bosom of that hill of Camulus,
Lo, purpled Cæsar, laurel-crowned, and legions.
The *scena*, a scaffold large, where, pictured round,
Much wilderness is, of Britain's field and wood.
Masque shall, of Britain's Orpheus, there, be played.
 Seemed then the choiréd Muses sit above,
In clouds, framed of the Isle's fine lawn ; and aye,
Those sisters nine seem Orpheus to inspire ;
Who, on a golden lyre, plays with his hands.
Seem, when, with clear note, like the heavenly
    lark,
He chants, the very forest rocks remove ;

Incline the stedfast oaks, to him, their heads ;
As pierced, by music, were their rinded ears.
　To him, outran, then, salvage naked brood,
Of men ; with whom leap beasts of several kinds ;
Forgot their wildness, from a painted grove.
Bears Orpheus also, in a mask of wood,
Such countenance, as seemed Claudius, in his youth.
Sith, all that brutish rout, that Satyrs seemed,
And pictured nations of cerulean Britons ;
Louting, in clownish sort, approached to Claudius ;
Loud hail him, Second Founder of great Rome.
　Still Orpheus chants :　and seemed blue warlike
　　crew,
Dance forth their mazy rounds, of vanquished
　　Britons ;
Treading strange wreathéd measures with swift feet :
He stayed his hand ; and run all back to wood !
Again he plays : those turn then, in new kind,
Now like a people of Gaul, *togata gens*,
Bearing, with Latin cries ! in, beams and stones ;
Wherewith they temple found, to godded Claudius !
Whereof large fundaments gin those cast around.
In midst whereof, is Claudius' *statua* seen ;
Which priests proclaim, is fallen, from stars, to-
　　night ;

And smokes, before him, incense, from the ground :
And all the army admire, and loud applaud !
  Then other four pass forth, like heroes clad,
Companions, on the earth, of heavenly god ;
Are friends to Orpheus, with high tragic tread.
Of the four tribunes, those bear visages.
And Aulus, all, and Geta and great Vespasian,
By name, acclaim ; by whom these things were done
  And, straight, is raised up, of some hidden engine,
(Minerva seems !) *Colonia Nova*, Claudia ;
Like shielded goddess, with high turrets crowned.
A sea-god's three-forked mace, her other hand
Upholds : and lead those heroes her to Orpheus.
And Orpheus' front, with leaves of bays, she binds.
Gan loud, then, Orpheus chant, with deeper note !
And the four dukes, with him, of manly throats ;
New Romulus, our *divus* Claudius,
Hath conquered, for great Rome, another
        world !
Then mightily all the army and long applaud !
So rise ; for trumps, to meat, call legionaries.
  In Colne's green leas, is portsale later made,
Without the dune, of weeping multitude ;
(Were they so many, that, is told, their chains
Had fraught a carrack :) who of tender age ;

THE DAWN IN BRITAIN

(Were crowned, with the field flowers, their innocent
    heads !)
And feebler sex, erst.   Seemed their piteous voice,
Cries of penned suckling lambs, and mother ewes ;
Which turn, heavy with milk, to fold, at eve :
When gin them herdsmen, with loud curs, divide.
To divers masters, parted from their babes,
Under the Roman spear, were mothers sold.
Sith captive men, of all blue Britons' tribes,
    Droves are, like pounded beasts, seen of bound
      warriors !
The most be those, (since, of this island nation,
Men wont not yield them to their adversaries ;)
Who smitten in battle-fields, and left for dead,
Were gathered, or else purchased, for base price,
Of Gaul's slave-merchants ; and sith, in the camps
Of legions, were those cured of their war-wounds.
Now slaves, at their vile list, them taunt and smite,
As their spears' captives ! Yond, in hurdle-
    pens,
Those stand ; they wait, (which, for their foster-soil,
Have bled, and Briton gods ; young drooping
    warriors ;)
Now, at a Roman outcry, in their own land,
Ah, to be sold ! Have merchants, from the Main,

Rich in this traffic ; young men of good stature,
Esteemed of price, apt to ward great men's doors ;
And should the more be sent, to marble Rome.
For now the merchant fleet shall sail, with Cæsar ;
To Gaul's mainland.   The imperial procurator,
Five thousand, the most tall war-hable youth,
Purchased for Claudius.   These should be reserved,
For that magnific triumph spectacle ;
Which shall make Claudius soon, in sovereign Rome !

Embarks now Cæsar, in high-pooped swift ship,
Of triple banks ; which urged of chosen rowers.
Cæsar takes Sabine ; who, of the blue Britons,
Can best great battle-shows devise, in Rome.
But come victorious Claudius, to mainland ;
By long paved street, he rides, in speedy chariot,
Now, towards Lugdunum ; city, in Togate Gaul,
Of his nativity ; (where him bare Antonia,
After her flight and fear, to Claudius Drusus.)
He, journeying, draws, the sixth eve, nigh that town ;
Whose noblest citizens, with the magistrates,
Be come forth, to third milestone, from their gates,
Of street called Sacra ; (which, on either hand,
Proud sepulchres border, of chief Gaulish houses,
Both of this city and the Romans' Province ;)

THE DAWN IN BRITAIN

With concourse great, to welcome Cæsar Claudius,
Whom all salute, Our great Britannicus!
  To Claudius, sith, much people, with the Senate;
Being come together, in their theatre,
Decree, with public games, triumphal arc;
And *statua*, with a golden Victory, winged,
In the *imperator* Claudius' high right hand.
  Upon the morrow, Cæsar wends, with pomp;
To altar of Augustus, twixt the streams.
And, lo, one purpled, by that sacred path,
Him waits, whose forehead girt with golden bend;
But, as murk twilight, be this stranger's looks.
And knew him Claudius, Herod Antipas!
(Was sometime tetrarch of a Roman province :)
Caligula him exiled. Is he that fox,
Which John beheaded : he whose ward of soldiers,
Spit on God's lowly Jesus; Whom they bruised,
Ah! and buffeted! and Him mocked, with sceptre-
    reed,
(Him, before worlds, ALL-RULER!) in his hand;
And diadem of sharp spines, and purple robe!
  Now this, which built Tiberias, by the Lake,
Dwells, in a Roman villa, by Rhone's stream;
Where, of an evil spirit, is vext his mind :
And his adulterous wife, and she him, hath

THE DAWN IN BRITAIN

In deadly hate.   Abhors this royal wretch,
In Gaul, each day's returning cheerful light.
   To Cæsar, bending, wisheth Herod gladness,
Of glorious Victory !   But ill omen Claudius
Deems salutation of this Jew ; nor spake
He word again ; nor will receive his boon :
But gathering up his purple, on his face,
Cæsar, impatient, hastes, by him, to pass.
   Were, three days, plays made, in their theatre ;
Where men, condemned to death, did fight with beasts.
The sixth eve, at Vienne, embarked hath Claudius ;
In barge, which falls, by day and night, down Rhone.
   To rich Massilia, Cæsar now arrives ;
Where mighty vessel, to receive him in,
With gilded poop, of many stories, lies.
That ship, by pulse is urged, of thousand oars.
The overmost, so are they great, be wrought
By wheels and pulley's force.   With martial pomp,
Claudius, the great Poseidon, goes aboard ;
For so is named this hull, that seems a town.
   Fair blows the wind ; and loosed from Gaul's great
      haven,
So they have towards Italia, prosperous voyage,
That the fifth eve, at Ostia, they arrive.
At dawn, behold, be come that city's Senate,

THE DAWN IN BRITAIN

To salute Cæsar : and him, laurel-crowned,
Convey.   Then, with them, Claudius rides to Rome ;
Where garlanded now all temples of the gods !
And thronging citizens, in her Sacred street ;
And banquets be set-out at every porch.
    Erst, in the *Curia*, a naval crown, Rome's Senate
Decreed to Claudius ; who Gaul's Ocean Stream
Had sent under the yoke ! and yearly games,
To memory of Isle Britannia's great conquest.
And be that haven, in Gaul, whence Cæsar sailed,
Adorned, it pleased, with high triumphal arc :
And be, of Roma, advanced, towards the North,
The city wall ; and Claudia the new port,
Therein, be named ; for Roma, upon that part,
Enlarged Britannicus !   Ending, then, new month,
Those captive thousands are, of wayworn Britons,
Come to the City Sovereign : through wide Gaul,
Scourged, like fierce beasts, their weary soles have
    marched.
Last were they, at Julii Forum,[1] stived in ships.
    Then Claudius, makes, for Romans, warlike
    games ;
In that large field, without their city walls,
This side the stream, by yellow Tiber's brinks ;

[1] Now Frejus.

THE DAWN IN BRITAIN

Which named of Marspiter, Rome's father-god.
Semblant prepared hath Sabine, of a dune,
In Britain, with her walls of wattled trees,
And stones and hoarded earth ; and wicker streets.
　　There Claudius, (now surnamed Britannicus,)
On set day, his war-spectacle shows to Romans!
Britons, with Britons, in two opposed bands,
Shall　fight　to　death.　　Two　thousand,　armed　as
　　　　Romans,
(Cæsar his freedom promiseth, to each one,
Which, in that battle, should have slain a man !)
Assail then, at third clarion : who within
Defending, glast-stained Britons ; till last won
The wall, all perish, in their burning town !

　　These things in Rome : but, in far Island Britain,
Unwist, to the proprætor, Aulus Plautius,
Is, whether yet live king Caratacus.
His Belges' spies affirm, 'scaped the war-king :
Other opinion hold, fell Britons' king,
In battle.　　Some mean, the king hurt to death,
Perished, mongst Camulus' burning citizens.
　　Being Aulus left, to end the war, in Britain ;
He, marched from Camulodunum, gathers tribute.
And, in the way; (where Cadern, magistrate,

THE DAWN IN BRITAIN

Of late deceased ; whose valorous son, Marunus,
Sore wounded, hardly saved was to far Ouse ;)
Submitted, to him, merchant Troynovant.
Aulus sends Flavius, then, to Cogidubnos ;
Confirm the Belges ; and all towns receive,
Which yield them, giving corn and hostages.
Being come down, by swift marches, to Longport ;
Warlike Vespasian, by night-time, embarked
His legion, passed that sea-sound to isle Vectis ;
Which full, he hears, of the war's fugitives.

And though, in Britain, verging be the year ;
Now entering, in the Scorpion, the late sun ;
Yet Flavius, in brief space, that isle subdued :
So turns, with infinite captives, to mainland.

Then led, by guides, through wilds of Durotriges ;
He assailed, out of the field, as they arrived,
From march ; and took the town, fair Moridunion ;
Whose king was fallen, mongst his proud warriors,
(Young valorous Golam,) under Camulus' walls.

In Britons' fields, where harvest-month now ended,
(Burned is earth's fruit ; or stands unreaped and lost !)
Falls rain incessantly ; wherefore might the Romans
Abide, no longer, under tented skins.
Then dukes, to winter-camps, withdraw their legions.

THE DAWN IN BRITAIN

Vespasian marched, to site commodious,
For corn and pasture ; where, amongst fair hills,
With temperate air, are certain scalding springs,
Of Sul, (Minerva of Britons,) healing goddess.

    There, lo, of sick folk, is an open dune,
Where wont, in bowers, those sit, all day, beside
Blue vaporous conduits, dipping oft their limbs ;
And drinking, oft, they snuff-up luwarm reek,
Casting-in gifts. Vespasian, now arriving ;
That none have fear, proclaims: who, from
    the war,
There wounded lie, shall yield their only
    arms.

    Entering, with reverence, then, the legions' duke,
Sul's temple-cave ; whence issues tepid reek,
Of boiling well ; great Flavius, to that goddess,
Sacellum vowed, and that of polished stones ;
If, by her virtuous spring, were healed his son,
Titus, hurt, in the assault of Moridunion.

    Concerning the well-bourn, and baths of Sul ;
Is told, in antique story, of certain king,
How, peradventure, he those waters found ;
Where opened had the soil, an heaven's lightning.

    Bladud, surnamed the Wolf, of those few lords
Was, which, from wars in Spain, returned with Belin.

THE DAWN IN BRITAIN

Come now from the Mainland, he homeward fares :
And Bladud journeying forth, in Britain, prayed,
To Belisama, his safeguarding goddess.
The king, one dawn, impatient forth to wend ;
Wight, of strange aspect, took him, by the hand,
The other, on his bridle royal laid !
   That Stranger's fashion was of shepherd hind ;
Yet more his stature, than the human, seemed.
Even so, it pleased transfigure her the bright goddess.
Nor he resisting, Belisama leads,
Where trooping sheep-flocks, scald with evil fare.
Through reeking well - bourn them the goddess
    drives ;
And they go healed up, on that further shore !
   Though looked he wide, then, in large field, and
    sought ;
King Bladud saw that herding-groom no more.
So lighted he, the virtuous brook, more near,
To view, down from his jaded steed ; which forth
Feeds, wavering from him, in the sappy grass.
But the steed, yonder, sliding, in much mire,
Fell, in that sheep-bourn : wallowing then uprose
He, all stained his bards ; but, shook him, with proud
    crest,
Loud neighing, unto battle and brood-mares.

The king, admiring ! in that bourn then cast
Iberian captive, all with long foot-march,
Fordone ; wretch, without hope ; which, this morn,
    was
By wayside, left ; where wolves, his abject corse,
Had rent, to-night : but, from that healing ooze,
Lifting, to heaven, his palms, thanking his gods ;
Revived, as in his youth, that captive rose !
    Bladud then, in the channel, washed his flesh,
Weary of long travail ; wherein, gins to creep
Now lustless eld ; and eftsoons the sire feels
His former pith renew, and warlike force ;
And, from his heart, is wiped all rust, even as
From a new-furbished glaive. He caused his ser-
    vants,
Then delve the bosom of that healing mould ;
And open conduits. Bladud timbered, sith,
Baths, for sick folk ; and himself there abode :
But SUL, name of the goddess of that ground,
Was to the slumbering king, revealed, in vision.
    Is this that Bladud, whom derne whispering voice,
Stirred, of familiar demon, in his ears :
Who tempting fly, from Troynovant, to the gods ;
In view of there great marvelling people's press,
Fell dasht, on Belin's temple-roof, to death !

THE DAWN IN BRITAIN

The prætor Aulus winters now in Kent.
His quæstor everywhere the Britons' corn,
Exacts, whose harvest lost ; nor mercy hath.
At his approach, him roused, then Dumnoveros,
Warden of Kent's shore, for Caratacus.
With all the remnant, of Kent's matchless scythe-
    carts ;
Crowned, with oak leaves, his brows, that sire rides
    forth.
    Leading swift chariots, he repulsed proud Romans ;
Falling, from thickets, on them, and hill-woods ;
And last, where streaming Medway would they pass.
And ever, mongst who foremost fighters, seen ;
Though bowed for eld and rheums, was Dumnoveros :
Till him swift dart attained, which his breast pierced.
His frighted steeds swerved, when the reins fell
    forth,
From his old dying hands ; and, in brier-bush,
Was caught the cart : they it shook, and broke the
    beam.
Tumbled that long-aged sire, and yielded breath !
Nor since was noised, deceased king Caradoc,
Desired he longer life : and fell his champions,
Him round, that sought save forth the royal corse.
Ere night, took Romans Durovernium walls.

THE DAWN IN BRITAIN

To Cæsar's arms, then yield them Lemanis,[1]
And Dubris, Cantion havens ; sith Anderida,[2]
To Plautius, last submitted Rutupîa ;
Wherein the widow of slain Heroidel weeps ;
Far from his own, who lies, a buried corse !
But Aulus sends a power, to Andred forest ;
To punish those hurst-dwellers, whom, in aid,
Caratacus hád called forth, to Camulodunum.
And are there mines of iron ; whence Britons armed,
He hears, were to the war : wold very great
And murk ; wherein, for latticed boughs, uneath,
Men pass : and archers climbed, from shroud of leaves,
Durst shoot, unseen, down shafts, on marching
    soldiers.
Fall many ; nor might Romans wreak their deaths.

But when had Thorolf heard, in Verulamion,
That great discomfiture, before Camulodunum ;
Nor hope rests, to renew the war, this year ;
And now the days, at hand, of winter tempest ;
Leaving five hundred helms, to Catuvelaunians,
And glaives, with all his spoils of arms and harness,
(Till come New-year,) to hold Cunobelin's walls ;
He leads, to Hiradoc, maugré horse of Romans,

[1] Lymne.   [2] Pevensey.

His hostings, through East March, to Branodunum :
Under whose cliffs, yet ride his dragon-keels.
    There they, with a loud Woden-chant, embarked,
Lift anchors ; and blue broad sail-wings up-hoise,
For Albis' mouth : where, Wittig, Thorolf hears,
Sits daily gazing from Forseti's [1] cliff,
To see his son's shield-scaled snake-ships sail home.

    But what seest thou, these days, O foster Muse,
Which all this land surview'st, in sacred Alban ?
    In Avalon, Joseph and the brethren saints,
Are fathers to all orphans of the war ;
And make resort to them, poor heathen souls,
As bees, to honey sweetness of Spring flowers.
Hath this year's harvest yielded, in the holms,
An hundred-fold.   Such is God's blessing there,
On Shalum, Christ's disciple's hands ; who hath
Enough, to nourish all who needy ; nor
The bitter cry is heard there, any more,
Of outlaws, who, for misery, ready were
To perish.   Joseph, Father-of-the-poor,
The Stranger, daily also, on the sick,
Lays healing hands ; and they recover health.

[1] A divine son of Balder and Nanna.

BOOK XVIII

ARGUMENT

Queen Embla, journeying with Caratacus, is now come down to Ouse: whither also the wasted army of North Britons arrived; and now return home. Maglos convoys sick king Caratacus, to his father, Moelmabon. Come to Caerwent, the lord sits in king's hall; where is, daily, much communing of the Roman war.

Idhig, Kynan and Maglos, march, in the next month, with king Caratacus. They fence an hill Eastward, against the nigh coming of the Romans. A daughter is borne to Caratacus. New pestilence, in the land. Come spring-time, Titus rides, with Roman sick, from Aquæ. They pitch, in Mendip. Titus daily rides an-hunting: he slays a monstrous wild swine. The *avanc* beast. He visits Alban, and finds the shipwrecked Syrians there.

Aulus builds strongholds, beside chief ways and at river-fords. Caer Isca is taken by the legions. Stratagems of Antethrigus; who lurks, in woods, to surprise the Romans' march. The warlord, in the Maiden's hill, laments his low and sickly estate. He leads his warriors, to another hill-strength; where, beleaguered by Aulus, he is delivered by the coming of Antethrigus. Antethrigus, hunted by Flavius, from hill to hill; and, at last, compassed-in, by his enemies, is slain. Soldiers fall upon an unarmed people of Britons. Who of them escaped, sail, with the Dumnonian king, to Erinn.

New parliament of kings. To them, unlooked for, comes the ethling Thorolf. Venutios, in vehement anger, hurls a

dart against Vellocatus, within the sacred close.   Thorolf is
recalled by his father's messengers, to Elbe-land, in Almaigne.
To him, sailing on the deep, Woden appears, by night.

Amathon cometh, with all his cattle, now to Alban.   Caratacus fortifies Glevum.   Aulus marches to assail the new dune.
In a tempestuous winter night, Britons unperceived, issue
forth ; and partly embarked in Kowain's ships they come
again, to Caerwent, unto Moelmabon.   Leaving his winter-
camps, Aulus journeys to Rome.   His ovation there.

A new revolt in Britain.   Beichiad, who had lain sick,
since the field of Camulodunum, marches in aid of his
brother, king Caratacus.   In the way, he sickens of the
pestilence.   Borne to his foster kindred, in the forest, he
dies there.

BOOK XVIII

Now, in what day was hurt Caratacus,
Fighting, warlord, before hill-dune of Camulus;
Whence were blue Britons scattered to far woods;
Who scaped, in chariots, drave still that night forth.
Who, gainst next eve, to willows of the Ouse,
Arrive; to pasture, loose their fainting teams.

North Britons, whom, (since fallen Velaunos,)
    leads
The king Venutios, marching, now fifth sun,
(War-wasted remnant of ere-thick caterfs,)
There pass; and lodge, few days, to heal their
    wounds.
Last cometh queen Embla, from Caer Camulodunum!
She, that still silent weeps, upstays, in cart,
King Caradoc: and cast dówn be all men's looks.
So drooping seems, so nigh the sire to death.
To Embla, druid leech of dead Velaunos,
Gives bitter herb, and certain infused root:

Whereof, when Caradoc drinks ; behold new warmth,
To him returns.   The king sate up, and shines
A lively hew, in all his god-like looks !
  But, sith blue Britons might no more, this year,
Renew the war ; and all their dukes have wounds :
Kings, (council held,) confirm were borne the sire,
For his more surety, now to Deheubarth.
  Passed forth Venutios, and those Northern powers,
New dread in Embla's breast, falls, of Gauls' horse ;
Which, the slow journeying of sick Caradoc,
Might lightly o'ertake : and she much Bericos fears !
  Known unto few, unfar, in a wide heath,
From hence, is, in some covert hollow place,
Mouth of deep winding and great cragged pit ;
Under this mould, whereon we mortals tread.
To that hid earth, now Embla turns aside ;
Whereof, by messengers, come from Antethrigus,
She knowledge hath.   With victuals' store and brands,
And archers' guard ; (those forest-wights which ward
Caratacus ;) she goes dówn, in that deep place.
  And, dwelling there, few days, both sense and breath,
Be come again, and favour of his face !
The queen then swift-foot runners sends, to Maglos ;
Who, towards West March, his stern Silures leads ;
Aye looking back, like boar that wounded is.

Him, in that midst, they found, where Cherwell's
    stream,
To Thames, runs down. And, heard their words,
    returns
The prince, with thousand hasting spears, to Ouse.
Come the sixth eve, king Caradoc and the queen,
(Whom there they find,) those bring forth. And their
    face
Now turned towards Hafren, warding the king
    round ;
They journey, softly, without any tarrying.

Ending that moon, they, to Caerwent, arrive.
Who lights, infirm, from wain, in rusty weed,
Worn, next his harness, but Caratacus !
Men joy, which see, returned their lord, alive,
From Roman field.   Wan is his royal face.
Lo Caradoc, drooping, leans, on his spear-staff,
And Maglos' hand.   They twain pass slowly forth,
With company and torches' light, in the lord's court ;
For fallen, already, is Britain's Winter-night.
The people, in king's hall, rise up, reverent.
Uprose Moelmabon, heard the purblind king,
Is Caradoc, of Cunobelin, coming in !
And, heavily, from his high seat he descended.

THE DAWN IN BRITAIN

To Caradoc, groped forth, on his aged feet ;
The sire him, goodly greeting, both his cheeks,
Kissed ; so asks of his health, and leads to sit,
In the high settle, with him : and commands,
Mix mead, bear ale anon, and set on meat.
But Nessa, white-armed queen of warlike men ;
Who lately, in Roman war, of valorous sons,
Bereavéd was, (put hastily off mourning stole ;)
Is, from king's hall, went forth, with maiden train ;
To welcome in, that now arrived, queen Embla.
So leads, with loving words, her, by the hand ;
Fordone, to women's bower, to sup, and rest.
Rest Embla ! and god-like, rest, Caratacus !
Sith, every day, the warlord's strength reneweth ;
And, in great mead-hall of king Moelmabon,
He sitting, of the Roman war communes.
And calls Silures' sire, in the long hours,
(That they, with some new thing, might light men's
        hearts ;)
His bards ; and tellers calls of evening tales.
Men number, on the fingers of their palms,
Lords fallen ; who with the foot, who with the scythe-
        carts ;
And that trimarch, which came out of North parts.
How, first, of Briton kings, fell valorous Golam ;

Mongst mingled mighty tread, of foot and horse :
Then that great lord, of all the Northern powers.
Riders of war-carts tumbled, rife, to grass,
In press o'erthrown of flying men and chariots.
Fallen, on his knees, was seen Segontorix :
Bellowing, like dying bull, he yet contended ;
And Atrebats, protending long swart shields ;
Made breastwork of their bodies still, gainst Romans.
  Duke Iddon's steeds, being early pierced to death,
Their traces, sunder-smitten, of bright glaives ;
Covering, with wicker shields, their woad-stained
      breasts,
Ten Catuvelaunian champions drew his chariot.
And, when one fell, another seized his room :
Whilst, beckoning, Iddon with his warlike hand,
(Midst immense din,) whereunto all obeyed,
Yet repulsed Romans ! till, (irruption made,)
A legion's cohort, that duke's cart cut-off.
Fell hundred round, nor took they him alive ;
For, in that moment, brast his mighty heart !
  Some tell of Romans' towers, and the elephants ;
And some of Erinn hounds, and bard Carvilios ;
Who voice, in Britain, was of battle-gods.
And how fell Fythiol, from swift battle-cart.
And how huge Ergund, rushing, with long lance ;

THE DAWN IN BRITAIN

(That a young poplar seemed,) resistless, burst
The legions' ranks : and when hurt Beichiad was,
And his companion-fighter hurt to death,
Ravished their madding team the rattling chariot.
Tell other, how, heard generous prince Marunus,
His father's death; and Troynovant, unto Romans,
Submitted hath; no more recovers health.
Is word, he passed hath winter-seas, to Thorolf!
    Moreo'er is told, of Ith, and men of Erinn.
Where Erinn's caterans rested, erst, in forest;
They invoked Neit.   Brehons, law-speakers, then,
And culdees, gave Ith read; that ended was
Now that behoof, which called them o'er to Britain.
And answered Ith, by Dagda, god that rolls
Night's starry round; they would return to Erinn!
    Long then their wayfare : is, in each wood-path,
Now venison their wild meat; and fishes oft,
Where rivers they mote pass.   They, journeying thus;
Sun see go down, in swart sea-waves, at length.
And being, untó Caer Segont, thence arrived,
They pass to Mona; and lodge on a salt strand,
Manannan's guests; who gives them sheep and beves.
    There Ith, and who kings with him and culdees,
Consult that oracle of old Samoth's god;
How windy sea-flood they, again, might pass?

THE DAWN IN BRITAIN

Then, neath broad-rising gleam, of second morrow,
Was wonder seen ! a thousand bascad boats,
Their former fleet, they left, on other strand,
(Power of blue watery gods, great Lîr and Nuth,
To whom, with vows, they prayed,) ride neath these
    cliffs !
Then softly breathed, in dead Carvilios' harp,
A wind ; whence being laid dark spirits of tempest,
That army of caterans safely overpass !

In the next month, came Kynan, Hammeraxe,
With Idhig, king of herdfolk Demetans,
Being neighbours both, to king Moelmabon's court.
Tells Caradoc, how, long-lying, in his trance,
He voice heard of some god, which him com-
    manded,
To build up Glevum,[1] gainst invading Romans.
Moelmabon king, in whom deep skill of arms ;
Whose wise breast full of memory of old wars,
It weighed commends, as counsel of a god.
He deems, fence, some hill-head, his March, to ward.
Accorded be those Western kings, in arms,
To fare, with Maglos and king Caradoc.
The fifth night of full moon, to Severn ford,

[1] Caer Gloew ; now Gloucester.

72

Shall they together come, with their caterfs :
Those homeward wend then, to their Winter-hearths.
The third night; when erst seen that new-moon's
    horns,
Young warriors, (come ere to their lords, in arms,)
Towards Severn marched; they find there, (with
    caterfs,
Whom Maglos leads,) warlord Caratacus,
Already arrived.   Britons then, uneath, pass,
For lifted Hafren's streams are on the land,
Full all, ice-cold, of frosty icicles.
    Four kings thence march, with six times thousand
    spears,
Through frozen woods ; so come, unwist of Romans,
To an hill-strength.   There delving Briton warriors,
With travail and long pain, for iron frost ;
That mount around, then, double rampire cast :
And wells, and pits, for harbour of their corn,
They dig.   Men fence them hardly from the cold,
With boughs of pine ; weaving thereof thick bowers ;
And sitting round, at eve, great common fires.
    Was tiding here brought, to king Caradoc ;
Queen Embla, his spouse, him borne a daughter hath :
Blue Britons name, then, with loud joyful crying !
The Maiden's Castle, that their Winter-hold.

THE DAWN IN BRITAIN

In Caerwent, night-time was of howling blasts,
And shrouded stars ; and frost lay on the ground ;
When gentle Embla heard her father's death.
She stooped, for grief ; fell on her childing pangs.
She prayed to Belisama ; and fervent asked
A son, like Brennus, to sustain Isle Britain.
Whispered the women-helpers of the queen ;
When, of a maid-child, she delivered was,
That her petition had not heard the gods !

O'er Britain's earth, hovers that homicide,
(With whom the demon-eagles, of four legions,)
Angel, well-pleased ! beholding, soaked with blood,
Of her own sons, and dunged with carcases.
Like evening's star, in misty heaven, I saw
Him, quoth the Muse ; or as seems, in men's seeing,
Oft-time, some noisome wayside puddle shine,
Like molten silver, neath sun's garish beams !
Cast a dire cry, that ever-damnéd fiend !
To hell beneath ; and called, from house of death,
Murrain, and Pestilence ; on all living flesh.
Their harvest-corn, not fully ripe, this year,
Was garnered ; grounden sith, in stress of war :
The very herb hath rotten gore infected.
Then erst, there perish multitude of beasts :

THE DAWN IN BRITAIN

Men die so many, in their poor hurdle-cotes,
Whom battles not consumed, inglorious;
That left is none to bury or to bear forth;
Or little earth strew on man's festering corse.
More than erst battle-gods, that sickness slays.
The ill then creeps in camps of Roman legions.
Caradoc and Maglos lead back their caterfs.
With dread, this Winter passeth, of all hearts.
But when the moon is in, of the new grass;
Flavius, from Aquæ, to the hills, sends forth
His sick.   Young Titus, who recovers health,
To Mendip, with them, rides.   Unto Caer Bran,
Then Romans come: old strength, and fenced with
       dykes;
Of Britons' former wars, a monument.
Those banks they entered; raise, therein, their tents.

The sickness hath allayed men's hostile hearts.
Titus deals kindly, with poor Briton folk,
Of these waste hills; and they again him praise.
And daily among them, he who hunting loves,
With few companions, bearing Gaulish bows,
Doth rouse the flying hart; or, mongst rough cliffs,
Thrills the grey wolves; or bays, in crooked denes,
The tuskéd boar, that rusheth on their spears.

Of certain monstrous swine, then Titus hears,
That harbour covert brakes, of yond wild crags ;
Whence she, in dale, the seeded plots doth waste :
And with sharp tushes, which be sickle-great,
That sow hath many hurt, and rent their hounds ;
And fall, like reeds, their weapons, from her crest.
One eve, as did they water their tired steeds,
By fenny brook, amongst brown bramble-brakes,
Outrushed, from thicket, that fell hideous beast,
Ox-great : her hanging dugs, unto the ground,
Did seem a battled wall ; and on whose nape,
And brindled chine, thick yellow mane upstares ;
Her eyes like coals.   Stept lightly, upon his feet,
The Roman knight, and poising swift iron lance,
He shot ; and twixt the shoulders, it gored deep,
The monster's flesh : that swine brake from them
    forth.
Mount hastily then the Roman knights, to horse :
Whose Briton steeds are wont, to these rough steeps ;
But twilight thickens on her bloody trace.
Last they all lighted ; and, now, tied their steeds,
They kindle fires and sup : sith, hunters, sleep,
Neath stars, on their spread cloaks, till morrow's break.
When drives new faery Dawn forth, in winged
    chariot ;

THE DAWN IN BRITAIN

And, from their golden manes, her rushing steeds
Shake dew, on the low earth ; and, to wide airs,
Her veil of crocus and her purple amice ;
Fleeing before Sun's face, she, virgin, casts
Upon the fleecy skies ; those knights uprose :
And ready, anon, they mount again to horse.
Titus bears Æthiopian bow of steel ;
Which only his young strength can ply, mongst
    Romans.
His messenger now it brought ; (whom he, to-night,
Sent back to camp,) with Briton hounds, in leash.
   In the fresh morning air, those questing run
Forth, on the blood.   Not long was, or their deep
Throats men hear open.   Romans, left their steeds,
Bounden, thrust-on, through thicket brakes, with spears ;
For now is roused the swine, from her night-lair.
    That sow outbrake, and rushed on men and
    hounds !
But her swift steel-head shaft attains of Titus.
She fell ; and wallowing rent the bloody grass,
And smoked the mould ; fierce hounds seize on her
    flanks.
The swine, of them, awhile, tormented was ;
Then last, with ferine groan, she gave the ghost.
   Sith, bear the brittled carcase Briton hinds,

77

(Poor wights, from herdmen's cotes ;) and crowned
    with flowers,
Their heads, with merry songs, and blithe reed pipes,
Up to Rome's soldiers' tents.   The monster's skull
They, and long red-bristled spoil, set on a pole,
Terrible to look on.   Britons there, to drink,
Remain : they eat with Flavius' legions' soldiers.
    Another while, strong comely Titus rides,
In the low plain, the *avanc* beast to hunt,
(Which, sithen, beaver hight, on English tongue ;
Fiber in Italy, where great Padus flows,)
Which timbers her, in fenny streams, an house,
Of beams, hewed with her teeth : whose floor she
    beats,
And pargetteth, with ooze, her chambered walls.
(Her hairy hide is holden good, for rheums.)
    Rides noble Titus, with few Gaulish horse,
And company of his friends.   Till noon, they naught,
Yet, find to hunt.   Would Titus then pass forth ;
Those Britons' sanctuary isles, beyond
The fen, to view ; whereof he heard, at Aquæ.
    Descended now, to Avalon's lyn, they find
A causeway of beams ; whereby, they overwade.
At Alban's borders, where white mere-stones set,
Britons meet Titus, with their magistrate ;

THE DAWN IN BRITAIN

Unto whom, (interpreting some Gaul with him,
Of the allies,) he peace, giving his hand,
And faith, confirms, of great Imperial Rome.
Titus, unarmed, then, enters with his friends.

Hyn erst leads Romans view, there, sacred pool,
Like crystal cup ; where men wont cast-in gifts.
Titus ring, from his finger casts, of gold ;
In saying, with voice of mirth ; To Britons' gods,
Behoves pay tribute! Who come, with him ; some
Cast pin ; some a *fibula*, or trifle of great Rome.

But when those light companions precious gifts
Perceive, lie glittering on that water's floor ;
Gold, silver vessail, sunk-up in base ooze,
Which, like scaled fishes, lurking under weeds,
The scattered sunbeams smite, whispering to Titus,
They him persuade, to break the Roman faith ;
And blowing trumpet, call in harnessed soldiers,
These things to reave. Reading their guileful looks,
Gather the innocent Britons covert stones,
In their poor weed. But straightway noble Titus
Rebuked, in the Greek tongue, his friends ; in whose
Hearts burns the hellish Roman thirst, for gold.

Then came an adder, with uplifted crest ;
(Whose scaly boughts, uprolled,) out of the reeds ;
And, hissing, fleeted on that water's face :

And Briton folk cry out, It is the god!
Whence, seeing them now much moved, made Titus
    haste,
To taste the proffered antique horn of mead ;
That fetcht is to him, from Sun's temple-house ;
Whereof, who drinks, men name him, sacred guest.
Hyn leads then noble Titus, to that hearth ;
Where, day and night, sits, venerable priestess,
To bete, with fenny turves, of Brigida pure,
Daughter of the Sun-god, the mystic fire.
Looked Keina, longwhile, on that knight of Rome !
Sith, stretcht her lean palm forth, in Britons' tongue,
Spake with loud voice ; and all, on Titus, gaze!
    Titus requires, What thing the Sibyl saith?
The Interpreter whispered, in young Titus' ears,
Thou, after days, she saith, shalt rule o'er
    Rome!
And Titus changed his colour, and shook out
His garments ; and made haste, to get him forth.
    Thence, Romans, rowed, in little wicker barks,
Be come to water-hamlet, in the mere,
Timbered on stages.   Romans, like to this ;
In that campaign, which Lucius made in Thrace,
Had seen.   Stand Britons forth, with brabbling voice :
They look askance, on strange approaching Romans !

THE DAWN IN BRITAIN

Hyn calls young Cuan, bard of the Cranog.
And seem when this on Erinn's trembling crowth,
Plays, sunbeams fall, as rain, on the dull mere.
Hearing his Briton chant, much like to song
Of birds, in leafy woods, admire the Romans !
Quoth Titus, Less could the immortal gods
Not, unto men that live, than these, have
    given ;
To whom are roots, he hears, of river reeds,
For meat; and fish, with honey of wild bees.
And yet, with golden music of the harp,
And warbeling chant, they live, as wanting
    naught,
Next to the gods.   And Titus silver brooch,
Which fastened had his baldric, gave that bard.

Yet, as they row from thence, is told to Titus,
Of certain strangers, which, in Avalon isles ;
Do lead their lives, in innocency, and in prayers.
And, lo, in holm, whereto they now arrive,
The man of God, who meets them, at the shore ;
Venerable of aspect, long, white-bearded sire !
On whom then looking, Titus, to his friends,
Whispers, as they again go up on land ;
Is not he like that Zeus of Phidias?
Which, in the Capitolium, now is seen.

THE DAWN IN BRITAIN

Albeit, go clad, in Briton weed, those men ;
Well, in the strangers' aspect, he perceives
That visage of the Jews, now many in Rome.
Hark ! Titus speaking, in Hellenic tongue,
And using the grave countenance of a Roman ;
Ordains, that they appear before duke Flavius !
Titus departing, spake ; Should Avalon isles
Be sanctuary still, and free from Roman
    tribute.

When issue Romans, now, from Winter-camps ;
Aulus erst measures long paved street, in Kent,
Which, on that conquered soil, he lays, like yoke !
Blue Britons, all, to servile tasks, unwont,
Labour, in bands, by cruel stripes enforced.
Strange insolent Romans, on them, now impose,
Nigh Samoth's cliffs, hew down their sacred groves !
Britons, war-captives, must fell holy trees,
Char coal, fire lime, delve clay ; burn Roman bricks.
They lay mule-loads, on Briton warriors' necks.
Makes each centurion levy, where he will,
Of the land's youth ; and shall those fight, as soldiers,
Beyond the seas, and die a Roman death !
Yet, Britons must endure, in name of tribute,
Grievous exactions, to be sent to Rome :

THE DAWN IN BRITAIN

Or of the quæstor's servants, infamous stripes,
Who cannot pay ; and yet it is not debt.

   When told these tidings, in the Maiden's Hill ;
Which newly, again, Caratacus hath beset ;
And purged, with fire and lime ; and wells, with pitch :
Standing, midst thicket, of tall glittering spears,
Great-voiced warsire of Britons, he set forth,
The intolerable wrongs of stranger Romans !
Have humbled them, in warfare, stranger
    gods ;
And weakened are the tribes, by pestilence ;
Yet when to bandy again, shall Britons' gods
Please, strange usurping soldiers to Main-
    land ;
Shall Gauls anew, them chace, beyond vast
    Alps,
And tread down Roma ; and Italy shall burn ;
And every nation take again her own !
   Builds these days strongholds, on both sides the
    Thames,
The legate.　But in forest, unsubdued,
(Where, to him, who most valorous of his part,
Come from East March : and in bowers of green
    boughs,

Those wonne, and under trees,) lurks Antethrigus ;
Whose wont is sally, unwares, on abhorred Romans ;
And kill, in night's thick murkness, and cut-off.
   Journeying now the propraetor unto Aquae,
Sends word, before, to Flavius, with his legion ;
To meet him in the path : which known to Maglos ;
Down from the Maiden's Hill, descend caterfs,
Twelve thousand spears, with king Caratacus :
And, suddenly, when a Summer day nigh ended,
Those, running, fall on Aulus' rearward cohorts ;
And on their carriage seize, and shrink the Romans.
   Then Aulus, on the morrow, in green plain,
Led forth, sets wide array, against the Britons ;
Hoping chastise those mingled loose caterfs :
But issues not, from wood, Caratacus.
   Then Aulus, ware and heedful, slowly marches,
Each day, few hours, exploring wide, with horse ;
And oft he halts, and must, with Britons, fight ;
That have each thicket-hill, beside the path,
Beset.   In that, warlord Caratacus,
Much dreading Romans should Duneda's town,
(For now their cohorts, by mid-Duffreynt, pass,)
Attempt ; before him urgent messengers sent,
To Isca.   Hardly were repulsed caterfs,
One noon, when Romans lodge ; and semblant make,

THE DAWN IN BRITAIN

Casting high bank, dig large their *castrum* fosse,
And deep : but silent, in that night's midwatch,
Left thousand fires, from decumanian gate,
The legate led, his legions' cohorts forth :
And, won ground of blue Britons, Aulus passed,
Beyond some perilous passage.   Yet, next night,
With guides, by moonlight, the propraetor marched ;
And outwent Britons.   Thence, young valorous
    Titus,
To that Dumnonian dune, he sends, with horse ;
To view the situation and the walls.
Rides, and turns, on the spur, by moonlight, Titus !
    Heard his relation, Aulus to the tribunes,
Commands, that, this day, rest within the *vallum*,
Their legions ; they, at changing of the watch,
To-night, shall march.   To captains of Gauls' horse,
Aulus prescribes ; at point of day, they were
The Britons' wall, so nigh ; that when, their
    cattle
And hinds and market-folk first, issue forth ;
They, in full career, might occupy the gate.
    Day dawns ; and now approaching Roman army,
Is seen from height of king Duneda's court ;
How, in low combe, thick-glittering cohorts march !
Journeyed, to-night, twixt Isca and the legions ;

Also Caratacus hath.   He blows grave war-horns,
On woody hill.   Duneda, heard that note,
With warriors, sallies from his river-part.
(Men hastily gathered, to the king, in arms,
Both of his own and warlike neighbour marches,
Which were not, in the field, with Caradoc.)
He stands, mongst their tall spears, in royal scythe-cart.
    Run forth, whom Kowain leads, stout Iscan youth,
From East-gate ; and hold shouting on, gainst
        Romans.
Come to hand-strokes, their left do wrest aside
The enemies' shields ; their fierce right hands stab
        soldiers ;
Or furious, on their bronze helms, sledge with stones :
And labouring reel the cohorts' ordinance.
    But cry, in that, went up, from the town part !
They looking back, behold their city's smoke,
As from a pot, above her bulwarks rise :
And breaks forth, lo, dread tumult, at her gates ;
Wherein they left their wives and little ones.
    Naught more hear words their ears, (nor heed their
        hearts ;)
Of who them leads : they turn their unfenced backs ;
And all, again, towards flaming Isca, rush.
They throng to gate, where terrible is now press ;

And Romans, at their necks, impetuous ride.
Few, that might enter, meet, in their own streets,
With Gauls' horse ; men that having fired the dune,
Themselves now flying, bear them through, with
    spears !
  Duneda riding, in one battle-wain,
With Hælion, stood in act to hurl his javelin !
When suddenly, split, under their feet, the chariot.
At the cross-wents, had swerved his teaméd steeds ;
Where, (grown now green,) is Mormael's mounded
    grave !
Howled hounds, steeds boggled ; the lord's axe-tree
    pight,
On some mere-stone : his lynch-pin brake, and
    strakes
And fellies were dissolved.   Sore bruised, on ground,
Lies, hurled, Dumnonians' sire.   Him, uneath, Hælion,
In mortal press, with flower of the king's champions,
Then saved !   The lord they lift, upon an horse.
His very hounds, to save the fallen sire,
Fight ; when fell, one on other, the king's warriors,
Under Gauls' spears, and glaives of expedite cohorts.

  Yonder, Caratacus battle joins ; leads Maglos,
With immense shout, Silures' rushing spears.

Those fall, like butting rams, on legions' cohorts.
But when Duneda's royal mount, behold
Britons, burn like vast beacon-hill, above ;
Their hearts stood still, within their straitened
    breasts !
And faint their knees ; looked even proud warriors,
Where might they save their weary lives, from death.
    Though god-like, yet, like brazen trumpet, shout
Sounds, bove the strife, of Caradoc ! fly blue Britons :
Ravished was, in their routs, even the king's chariot.
In vain the warlord, feeble of his hurt,
Leans forth ; and heartens still, with voice, blue
    warriors !
Fast, áfter them, pursuing then bloody Romans ;
Is Isca field left empty, with her dead !
    How smokes that goodly great dune royal ; rich
With shipfare, and tin-traffic to the Main :
High seat, of druids' veiled antique discipline !
Great was that victory of the Roman legate.
    Wander, as roes, and tremble, in the fern,
Of summer woods, her drooping fugitives.
Journeying hurt king Duneda, in war-wain ;
Ere dawn, raught to dune-hill of Amathon.

    Aulus, moved by commodity of the site,

THE DAWN IN BRITAIN

For corn and herb and water, for his horse ;
And by the amenity of this fair Duffreynt,
Will stablish, at Caer Isca, stative camp.
    But erst, (and having his commandment left,
Isca's high walls, lay even with the ground !)
With horse and knights, lo, Cæsar's legate rides,
And Flavius, and who præfects of his legions ;
Till, to that Bloody Foreland, they arrive ;
Which End of Land.   There seemed-them see the
    sun
Sink, hissing, in dim bosom of vast Main !
    And, where he passed their marches, he received
Moon-shield Belerions, to be under tribute.
Decet, long-languishing, of a javelin-cast,
Which opened all his chest ; (and, fallen from cart,
Their king, his shoulder broke, when Antethrigus
Was smitten, by Thames ;) is newly there deceased.
    Sith sacrificed a sow, to Hercules, Aulus ;
And set up trophy, of his enemies' arms ;
On that last head-of-land, which looks toward Erinn :
With superscription, to Rome's gods and Claudius !
And glorious letters, thence, indites, to Cæsar,
Prostrate South Britain, ended is the war.
Pitcht, at dim Western sea-rim, stands his
    tent !

THE DAWN IN BRITAIN

He sends, returned to Isca, expedite cohorts,
With certain Gaulish horse, to Amathon's march :
His hope is gather there, both corn and victual,
Of cattle.   But now those Britons their hill-dune
Have burned, and wide field wasted ; and were driven
Their sheep and great horn-beasts, to Pedred Fen ;
Beyond pursuit, for quavemires and blind moss ;
And where ben known, to few, the marish paths.

Now when the Icenian hero, Antethrigus,
(Who lurks, still, in green forest, unsubdued,
And meditates, aye, new warlike stratagems,)
Had word, of cohorts' camp, that gather tribute ;
He wicker maunds, on chines of hundred beves,
Lays ; wherein he twice hundred champions hides ;
And with them he sends other, that seem hinds ;
Drivers, with skeans bound, neath their blanket-bratts.
Again young Madron is their hardy captain.
  Some wend before, in guise of Dobuni :
And these allege, come to the camps of legions ;
For carriage of the tribute-corn, and drift
Of thousand beves ; except by covert night,
They durst not journey, for Caratacus.
  Those droves, come, in dim night, to *castrum* port ;
Suffer centurions of the watch, to pass,

Beves' train, tumultuous.   Light them some ones
  forth,
Whereas the tribute-grain, borne on their beasts'
Chines, they might, in the open place, discharge.
Lappęd, in their saies, come shivering Roman soldiers,
From leathern tents, (now chill is the night season ;)
For joy, see all this victual.   Covert word,
Spake Madron !   Suddenly those stout drivers, glaives
Drawn, in fierce heat ; then smite unready soldiers !
Men, from those double maunds, now leap to ground !
An hundred and an hundred, tall armed champions ;
Chace then the oxen, bellowing, furious ;
Which, on their wide-embowéd horns, bear forth,
And trample, as cockt hay, the tents of soldiers !
Britons, with dreadful yells, all, rushing, slay,
That come within their hands, to the camp-walls ;
Where, (like as ploughman, at his furlong's end ;)
Drive, their fierce beasts about, those Briton warriors.

  The cohorts' watch, which fight against them, there,
They overrun.   Being come to *vallum*-port ;
They slay, themselves, their beves and choke the gate,
With carcasés ; that might not soon Gauls' horse,
Thence, after them, pursue.   A score, no more,
Be fallen of East-men ; but run down, with sweat,
Their warlike limbs, and ache their strong hand-wrists,

Of their much vehement smiting ; whilst, of Romans,
They, in their camps have slain, the souls descend,
To their pale sires, that tremble yet, for Brennus.
　　But fight on, in their *castra*, legionaries,
Supposing were their foes all, in night murk,
Which of strange speech.　Smite Romans their allies,
(Gauls and Batavians.)　Last, when morrow breaks,
Gathered　their　slain ;　they　bury,　as　twelve-score
　　soldiers !
　　Yet Antethrigus, where should cohorts pass,
Lays ambush in a wood.　Half-backward, hews
He trees, beside the path ; and knits long ropes,
Unto their leafy cops : in other trees,
He archers shrouds.　Sith, enter train of soldiers ;
That having, all day, under heavy arms,
Gone, in this Summer-heat, much thirst and sweat.
And　some, (none　enemies　seen,) their　helms　have
　　doffed ;
And cast in wains, (that bring their heavy stuff,)
And shields and harness.　They, with ribald songs,
Of their rude throats, disordinately march.
　　A woodwale shrieked ! at that sign, from the gods ;
Was dreadful sudden noise, in Roman ears !
Of rushing forest ; whose stiff crooked arms,
Whole companies strew, at once, beat-down, oppress !

THE DAWN IN BRITAIN

Tumble green groves, about men's fearful ears ;
That felled are, on the mould, whelmed, dasht to
    death.
Who rest, cry out ; This wood's gods fight with
    Romans !
Titans, which hurl, down on them, leafy
    towers.
Is death, midst rushing beams, by Britons' shafts.
  Faber proclaims, who this relief of soldiers
Leads ; that, for every Roman slain, he will
Kill now two Briton captives, in their seeing,
That shoot ! But those, lo, their gyved hands up-
    holding,
Do loud protest, they spare not, for the gods !
For them to die, (which have lost all,) were
    light.
Come lateward Romans forth, with grievous loss.
  Heard Antethrigus, that new cohorts marched,
From Aquæ ; he cast those bathed and perfumed
    Romans
Enwrap ! He sends some, of his vowéd champions,
(Men, that, with oaken leaves, and whistered words
Of druids, have bound their brows, to Camulus ;
To further Britons' war, with their souls' deaths !)
Like fugitive thralls. With well-dissembled tale,

THE DAWN IN BRITAIN

Whilst those hold speech, mongst who, in Ikenild,
    Street,
With spades and axes, open, pioneers,
Wood-path, before the marching legionaries;
One cometh, their tribune, clad in purple weed.
But falling, in this Roman's mind, suspect;
He his soldiers charged, Attach them! which
    perceiving,
Britons, pluckt their skeans forth, would there have
    slain
That Roman duke; and one smote-through his horse.
He fell; but shield him soldiers, with thick spears.
Britons die, having each one slain a Roman!
    Weary, in rain, cast Romans, round them, bank;
Wherein they lie down, fearful, in their harness:
And cry, from man to man, the time of night;
Till morrow break. Thenceforth, those Romans
    march,
More circumspectly; and when now woodland, large,
Before them, lies; they bind their Belges' guides.
    There, tramelled, find they, passage of all paths.
Soldiers, by shafts of unseen foes, fall pierced.
The tribune sounded clarion then, Knit shields!
So come they, foot by foot, rank behind rank;
None having turned their backs, from forest forth.

THE DAWN IN BRITAIN

Returned king Caradoc, to the Maiden's Hill.
Now night, by watchfires of sweet smelling pine;
Hewed as the poplar leaf, he, king of warriors,
Sits, mongst his long-haired captains; that deposed
Their helms, and arms laid by their valiant hands;
At chequers play, on bulls'-hide long, war-bruised,
Hard shields. But nothing list, in stress of war,
To play heart-weary Britons' sire. On stars,
The hero's eyes be fixt, which men call gods:
And bitter seems that mead-cup Gorran bears.
He cry aloft, of dreary night-fowl, hears;
That flit from carcases unto carcases!

To gods, on height, that in yond heavenly towers,
Dwell, as men ween, in an eternal feast,
Of youth and ease, and light and divine force;
Lifting his eyes, laments king Caradoc,
His sickly estate. He cannot now, as erst,
Fight, from his scythe-wheel, swift-teamed, battle-
    chariot.

He left alone is, in Cunobelin's house.
His Catuvelaunian royal state is lost;
Is taken Caer Verulam, Camulodunum burned:
And, after war, hath entered pestilence.
He marvels; why, (now harvest-night!) yet, comes not
Thorolf? Will Summer-season soon be past!

THE DAWN IN BRITAIN

He hears his lords commune, how Antethrigus
Useth war-stratagems : but the martial son,
It likes not well, of great Cunobelin.
Received have Catuvelaunians, of their sires,
By open valour, smite their enemies.
   Late, the self night, from fever dream, awaked ;
Because him token had given his fathers' gods,
By ravens ; that must Romans win this strength,
Caratacus roused his warriors to remove.
And, lo, from thence, at dawning ray, descended ;
They champaign wide, to new hill-fort, o'erpass ;
Whose foot in Yvel stream : and, triple banks
Digged round, that ward will hold Caratacus.
   When hardly is this full-ended, Roman cohorts
Approach, with Aulus.   Leaguering, round the
     mount,
Soldiers, by day and night, labour to turn
Fair Yvel's stream, from the now shut-up Britons :
And when, night-time, those and their beasts, must
     drink,
Romans shoot, on them, stones, from wain-borne
     engines ;
And thirst, in their own land ! war-weary Britons.
   But when hath Antethrigus word thereof,
Through spies ; he, with his East-men, hastily marched,

THE DAWN IN BRITAIN

From Coit Mawr [1] forest. They, to succour Caradoc,
Contend.   And now, as mountain wolves, by night;
Those come, to hindward of the legions' *vallum*,
Blowing loud hundred war-horns! clamour raise;
As many bands did, in vast field, arrive.
Whilst soldiers then much doubting, in dark watch,
Standing in ordinance, keep the *castrum* walls,
Caradoc; whom Antethrigus had forewarned,
Closely, unmarked of Romans, ere that star,
Which, messenger of new day, again, is risen;
Led his blue warriors, from the hinder part.

Romans, sent scouts, at dawn, find Britons' camp,
Empty: but sith, when hears the Roman legate;
How now, to Pedred fen, Caratacus
Was went; leaving the war to end, to Flavius,
On this side Thames; he, duke, with his most horse,
Returns himself, to Roman Troynovant.

Vespasian, taking certain expedite cohorts;
Then they, from hill to hill, like salvage beast,
Valley to valley, Antethrigus hunt.
But that great Briton, some, to spy out Romans,
Sends, like base herdfolk, clad, in pilches rough;
And bearing slings and hurl-bats their tough hands.

These leasings sow, mongst hungry Roman Gauls;

[1] The Great Wood, in Somerset.

THE DAWN IN BRITAIN

How, from the Summer-pastures, had they driven
Much cattle down, to green plain.   Browse their horn-
    beasts,
Yond, the late herb, within a valley's mouth.
Persuaded of them, many Gauls then ride.
Passed league's way, those hear lowing now of kine,
Whither they come, within a cragged cliff.
    They throng in; but beyond, in cumbered place,
Of thorns, which haunt sweet birds, and trickling rocks;
The skies did seem rain on them, shafts and darts.
Then would those Gauls, betrayed, fast backward ride ;
But kindled foes, against them, have all thicks !
Now, leaping dire, wild flames run on the ground ;
Dance dread, uplifted, roaring, on the wind :
Them chace, which way they turn, with open throat.
    Who, half-scorched, flying from this fiery death ;
Fall on great felled trees, that bar now the path,
With their stiff crooked arms.   Pursue fierce Britons,
With fearful yells ! and iron and thrilling bronze.
    Five only of Romans win, again, to camp :
Then damned be those few Britons, to the death ;
Which, for a pledge of faith, were there left bound :
But they, empaled, did glory, in their bold deed !

On pallet lies Duneda, in Pedred, bruised.

THE DAWN IN BRITAIN

The old king, oft, in dreams, beholds a god ;
Him beckoning unto soil of Sacred Erinn ;
Land of the dying Sun, that Second Britain.
Wherefore, interpreters called of visions, druids ;
Sith fair Duffreynt lies waste, and Isca burned;
The king, (dune, where dwelt his old royal sires,)
Is minded, sorrowing, o'er West seas, to pass.
    Moreo'er hath sent now Ith, to kings in Britain,
His message ; should, in Erinn, fields be given,
To Britons, which would flee Rome's servitude ;
Esteeming riches, not to live oppressed.
    Then banned, is, in all borders of Duffreynt,
That king Duneda fares to Soil of Erinn,
To sojourn there, till gods, expulse strange
        Romans.
Come; whoso would, with king Duneda, em-
        bark,
To him, at Aber Kambilan, with their stuff!
    Now, when heard Flavius, of there gathering
        Britons ;
The duke, with speed, returns, from Antethrigus :
But, with oft onset, of swift hovering scythe-carts,
Troubles the hero each Roman march ; till, last,
He was bewrayed, of Belges, where he is :
For had a price set Flavius on his head.

Vespasian compassed, sleeping then in grove,
Him, and his champions ; where no water was.
Being come day's heat, is fought, with hurled-out
        javelins.
But Flavius, that none enemies scape thereout,
His soldiers hath, commanded, dig ; and bank,
Around them, cast.   Romans and Britons strive,
Till eve ; when now blue warriors thirst and faint :
Falls sith a dew, which somedeal them refreshed.
    Now slumber soldiers ;   which, in haste, have
        supped ;
Without the cast of slings and shot of darts.
Only the watch, with glaives strained in their hands,
Listen each bruit of the forest leaves !
    Stand Britons, waiting sign of Antethrigus,
Now, in wood-side, all ready to leap forth :
Waits the hero, on an omen from his gods.
Flits a wood-howlet ! and the dusk night thwarts,
Before the fierce eyes of strong Antethrigus.
Then that great Briton, certain now of death,
Rent oaken leafy bough ; and bound his span-
Wide front therewith : hark, imprecation makes
The hero, to his gods ; for Britons' health,
Vowing his body and blood, to Camulus !
    Smiting then palms together, he gave sign ;

And first, with long bright glaive, breaks forth on
    Romans!
He fell out on them, as stoops hawk from cliff:
And seemed, in that he o'erleapt his enemies' dyke;
Some battle-god, with lightning in his hand!
East-men hurl javelins, which, in their murk grove,
Were fallen.   From the two parts, Vespasian's
    soldiers,
Whom clarion wakens! uprisen; run, in harness.
They hem, they Britons close-in, at their backs.
This glory give to Flavius, Roman gods,
Take so great barbare captain; on whom, next
To Caradoc, leaned the estate of all South Britons.

    Is told, when drunken was his desperate blade,
With slaughter blood, and he himself hurt oft,
Of darts; as he pursued a helm-bright Roman,
In that the moon, from dim skies, shone a moment,
With low and little light; the hero's foot,
In corded beechen root, latcht.   Rusht, woeworth!
To ground, he, ón broad targe, and on his face,
And lay full still.   He, parted from his own,
For loss of blood, faints mongst his enemies!

    On Antethrigus' neck, leapt harnessed soldiers;
And on his mighty limbs, and his large chest!
And they him, back and side, anon, have pierced.

THE DAWN IN BRITAIN

Is none, of all that brave him round, with dart
Or glaive, is in his hand, which doth not hurt,
To death, great enemy, dying Antethrigus!
Who gave, with groan, the ghost. Lifted, some one,
Last those long yellow locks, his head offsmote.
  Though, from his shoulders, the grim · poll be lopped;
They stare, with fear, still, on his threatful face;
Whose barbare blue eyes, dazing now in death,
Seem adders, that gaze from some baleful bush:
And ring-gold seemed the hero's ravelled locks;
And like to harvest shocks, his side-long beard,
Unkempt; for Antethrigus kept his oath.
And was, in days of great Cunobelin,
And of his warlike sons, the Britons' wont;
That freeborn men, and all of warlike age;
(Save the lip-beard, in token of Camulus,)
Go shaven-faced. Lo, on a pole, borne forth,
That mighty head of East-land's magistrate,
Seemed tawny jowl of boar, with hideous mane.
They crucify the hero's corse, whose stature,
Exceeds that, by two spans, of any Roman.
  Not many, of East-men's champions, scaped that night,

The Romans' glaive.   They few, was overmatched,
Their valour and great force, of numbers' weight.
Yet some, next night, returned ; from Roman cross,
Stole body ; and bury, of gréat slain Antethrigus !
   Sith, on much journeying foot-folk, to Duneda,
Come nigh to Camel-mouth, fall Flavius' soldiers.
In that inglorious victory, of Roman cohorts,
Over an unarmed barbare multitude, was
Gathered much prey, of weed and ornaments.
   Who scaped, lamenting, from the Gaulish horse,
Embarked, with king Duneda, in many ships.
The weeping Britons, as they drew up sail,
Prayed their sea-gods, that might they safely pass !
   A second day, they welter, in West deep :
Then touch their prows, to soil of Sacred Erinn.
Descends the sire Duneda.   Is Westing now
Sun to world's brink ; and seems wide firmament
Pavilion, lo, of purple and fine gold,
Of Erinn's gods.   Then first, with covered head,
And stretcht forth his washed palms, he, reverent,
      them
Salutes, which have here name of chiefest gods.
Sith demons of the ground, air, floods and woods,
And well-springs.   All then, leap out of their prows,
His people, unto shore of this new Britain !

THE DAWN IN BRITAIN

Now ; and for not possible were renew, this year,
The Roman war ; with Maglos and caterfs,
Ships, from an isle, erst tongue of land, warlord
Caratacus : for whilst, behind their steps,
They digged, to fence them from their enemies ;
It so, inrushing tide, deep channel made,
(And seemed then fight, for Britons, Eagor, god !)
And wide ; there might none Romans overwade.
Sith lords and warriors, in Duneda's ships,
To Caerwent sailed ; return, to Moelmabon.

Thence Caradoc sends to North and Midland kings ;
Bidding them come, to him, to certain place ;
Which great stones compass-in, by Upper Hafren.

Now kings and lords, together, there arrived ;
Sit down, in circuit, with Caratacus.
Comes lateward to them, here, divine Manannan ;
Ridden on his mule, from Mona, by hill-paths.
Unlooked for, last, came, from beyond seas, Thorolf !
Marched with stem-fighters, only, of two ships.
By word of Veleda's mouth, the prophetess ; wars,
Which lately had king Wittig, were composed.
From Elbe-mouth, boldly then, in Winter-season,
The ethling sailed ; and steered towards Island
    Britain :

Where would he see, (great kinsman of his house,)
How Caradoc fares. Touched land, in Meltraith Fleet,[1]
Those Almain prows ; whence he, with guides, ascended,
Through fens, through woods, of East and Midland Britons ;
Where, new built, not few strongholds, he, of Romans,
Beheld ; by fords' heads, and land-passages.
   Thorolf, his homicide spear, (for none might armed
Enter that doom-ring,) hath, and Brennus' blade,
Without ; and Weyland's moon-sheen targe, deposed.
All loud salute that royal glorious Almain,
Who now arrives !   And he again them greets.
And Thorolf sate down, by Caratacus.
   Propounds sith Thorolf, his heroic thought ;
Come to him, sailing on sea-billows hoary ;
Trine daughters of East wind: Fence all South Mark,
Twixt Hafren flood and dune of Camulus ;
Calling armed multitude in of Brennid Almains !
   Who then, to this, persuades but Vellocatus ;
Uprising, mongst them, radiant as a god !

[1] The Wash.

Whole now his hurt : and being his father, Cotus,
Lord of the parts of Derwent, newly dead ;
Is he a king of fair Brigantine March.
   Gainst whom, incensed, with fierce heat, king
      Venutios,
(Aye, and with prophetic spirit of things far-off,
Instincted, of the ever-living gods !)
Outcries ; him naming public enemy!
That would new stranger arms call in to
      Britain.
Have not Iceni expulsed an Almain fleet,
From harbour, at East cliffs? for were they
      pirates!
   Then seeing, how proudly him bears his adversary,
Not longer the old wárrior might refrain him ;
But risen, enflamed with felon heat, passed forth :
Where snatcht, from hand of one of his, a dart ;
He it hurled back, sudden, in that hallowed close !
Midst lords and Britons' kings, and sacred, druids :
And murmur rose, among them, for that deed.
   Venutios would have slain false Vellocatus ;
But erred his pulse. The violent iron flew forth,
Eager drink blood : on pillar-stone it pight ;
Where, ware-eyed, Vellocatus' hand it caught ;
Who nimbly upleapt, in time, had bowed to side.

THE DAWN IN BRITAIN

Full of resentment, this, before them all,
The young king shows! Bear witness lords, he
     cries ;
He, guiltless man, doth now, in fine, renounce
All legiance, to law-breaking lord Venutios.
Seeing the moon eclipse, all fear that night.
     Lo, kings, with pomp, the third day after this,
Of their armed folk and shrill war-carts part forth ;
Being all accorded, with king Caradoc,
Renew the Roman war. They, in Lent month,
Should gather, to him, armed, with new caterfs.
     But, in one chariot, with Caratacus,
Returning thence, was stayed the ethling Thorolf,
By messengers at the watering of the Theme ;
Almains, come in longships, with speedy oars :
And voice pronounced, of him who leads them,
     (Hiradoc ;)
Invade, Lord, Elbe-land other enemies!
     Thorolf then, thrice, embraced king Caradoc ;
Whilst each calls other Brother ! and kissed, thrice,
On both his cheeks. The ethling parts, in haste :
The Almain hero's heart presaging ill,
By neighing of his steed. Misgives him, he
May no more tread Bret-land, in arms of Brennus!
So, sorrowful, he returns towards that sea-haven.

THE DAWN IN BRITAIN

There he inships.   His sea-carles row : now hoise
Blue wadmel sail, (wherein king's broidered token,
Gold-bristled boar !) on hoary Winter-deep ;
In whose wild tumbling surges, aery spirits
Seem   dance   forth,   of   West-wind :   but   Thorolf's
    keel,
Proudly, the heaving billows overrides ;
And tosseth to each part, her wingéd breast.
    Who, to this shipfare, sends him merry breath ;
(Wherein giant Fasolt,[1] of the watery storm,
From land, before him flies, to the fast land,)
The mighty Lord-of-spells, King-of-the-slain,
High-father of his house, alwitty Woden ;
In his sea-sleep, shows Wittig's glorious son,
The late days of Earth-world ; to go before
All-doom, and last death of long-living gods ;
How all must be subdued, to fatal Rome !
    Vain thing, to turn back the decree of heaven,
Were the effort of a man ; though he most valorous,
In counsel and in force.   The god, to Thorolf,
Makes   known,   Him   rest   few   now,   but   glorious
    days :
So   the   three   virgin   Norns   shaped,   at   his
    birth ;

[1] Gigantic wind-god.

So twined their hands; so spent, from East
    to West,
The golden thread, in heaven, of his life's age!
His   seed,   nathless,   should   herit   land ⋅ of
    Brennus.

    Came Amathon, in those days, to fenny Alban.
His cattle were driven before him, and much corn
Borne in his wains ; for was he not to Erinn
Fared, with Duneda : but the sire in land,
(Died Bara in the late pestilence ;) would end,
Which nourished hád him, his fathers, and their flocks.
    Hyn gathered then young men : which withy rods,
Lopped in mere-side, have pilled; and now those pight
Long studs, in compass, (nigh to Brigida's house,
The place ;) do wreathe there hall, of hurdle-work,
For this good lord, with wicker bowers ; and thatch.
    Behold, that venerable sire, in holm,
Host of the saints, now dwells, of sacred Avalon !
And   communes   oftwhiles   Amathon,   with   Christ's
    brethren.
Sith when long nights be come, of Winter-season ;
And all without lies cold and comfortless,
To Cuan hear, him pleaseth passing well.
    Are Cuan's dreaming strings, in this lord's ears ;

Like to that golden murmuring, which of bees,
Sounds mongst sweet linden boughs, in the Hay-
    month.
And Dylan, hind, which erst, with his two sons,
Received Christ's messengers, saved to Britons' land ;
In osier cabans, wonne their lord around.
    King Caradoc dwells, in Caerwent, with Moel-
        mabon,
Two months ; (where bands, come, of his Verulam
    warriors,
Now, in nigh forest, build them Winter-bowers.)
Like space, he dwells then, with the sire Manannan,
In Mona, in his new hóuse ; which overrides
The path ; that needs must enter all which pass,
Under his roof ; where tables, ready-dight,
Stand ; set with meat and drink, for all who list.
And bards, remembrancers, in the sire's hall,
Sing, each eve, lays, which made Carvilios ;
Like to war's blowing trumps and rushing chariots.
    And come in weaponed youth, to the lord's
        hearths ;
To hear war-speach of king Caratacus.
For tales of mirth and solace, cure their hearts,
No more, nor heed, of jesters, the light parts ;
Whose words were shafts of laughter, in men's ears ;

Nor they love-longing's dulcet idle note,
List, or bard's chant, that breathes not bloody war ;
Nor any, in treacherous metheglin, drencheth more
His sense : but sounds, with din of smitten arms,
All day, their craftsmen's street ; where Caradoc
    walks,
With Ergund prince, wounded at Camulodunum.

    Fell Winter, which the land hath lately wasted,
And spoiled of weed ; now holds her, shrouded corse :
And wall of darkness seem the skies above.
Dead seems the world ; save where the wild waves
    break,
And rushing tempests, in the aery paths.
    In those days, rose up warlord Caradoc,
In Caerwent, with the sons of Moelmabon ;
And leading youth of Dyved,[1] tall caterfs,
To Caer Glew, (dune of Dobuni,) now they march.
    To river-isle, they Severn overpass :
Where come ; they, for Corinium, burned and waste,
Will wall-up a new dune ; wherein, well-fenced,
West Britons might safeguard their souls, from
    Romans !
Labour Silures warriors, delve deep fosse

---

[1] Demetria, or South-west Wales.

And wide; and it with stakes beset.   The dyke
Those crown, with pales.   They lead then, in their
    work,
Clear Hafren's stream.   Last timbered they tower-
    gate.
  Thereon Caratacus set up image bright,
Of Britons' battle-god, swart Camulus :
Which Embla saved ; when she king Caradoc, sick,
Saved, from that sieged dune, in a covered cart :
Unto whom, might warriors, entering into fight,
Pray and look dying, on his glittering face !
Whilst thus they wrought, the Winter now is past.
  Returns the lengthening month, of the new leaf :
When Roman captains, from their Winter-camps,
Lead forth the cohorts.   This year, their hope is,
To conquer all West March ; though, in the Pro-
    vince,
Be tumults ; where yet yield not to be tamed,
Tribes that pay tribute.   Britons, which revolt,
Look daily, that should come king Caradoc :
And say, drawn of white steeds, by time of
    night,
In forest, was the warsire seen to ride.
  Pass moons ; and erst, when Summer well-nigh
    ended,

THE DAWN IN BRITAIN

Is told to Aulus ; how Caratacus hath
Dune, in an isle, midst streaming Severn, fenced ;
And stored with arms and victual. Marched from .
    Aquæ,
To Glevum, then, with cohorts of two legions,
The legate.   There, hewed alders in the plain,
He bridge builds ; and towers timbers, for his engines,
Of siege : and Romans leaguer, round the walls.

    Beyond all former wont, that siege endures ;
What for the valour of defending Britons,
Their rampire's strength ; and they have learned, as
    Romans,
Neath tile-work, now, to fight of knitted shields :
And fenced, with wattle breastwork, be their walls.

    There warlike women oft, men's weary watch,
Relieve ; nor when lack bowstrings, any spares
Her own bright locks, to shear, as wiry gold ;
To Deva, the white goddess, of clear Hafren,
Commending her ; whom she, with often gifts,
Serves.   Some, with lily fingers, long and small,
Twining their hairs, plight nets.   Salmon those, then,
Take, in large seine, which sends, in the cold stream,
In scarcity of the siege, the river's god.

    The warsire never ceaseth from the walls :
And sallying Maglos oft, like vehement flood,

THE DAWN IN BRITAIN

With his armed youth, surprises and slays Romans.
Those, day and night-time travail, till month ; when
Must drive them, from their tents, the cold and rain.
   Romans, which privily have burrowed, neath their
     fosse
And dyke ; sith pierce within blue Britons' work.
They then, in night, tempestuous, feign assault,
On further part. As moldwarps were, from earth,
Uprose few harnessed soldiers ; and those wind
Loud clarions, now, in Glevum's market place !
Which entered, in king Caradoc's dreaming ears ;
Who late lay down to slumber, at the walls :
The warlord leapt, upon his feet, in arms.
   Then longed his soul, as bridegroom for the night,
In twilight of these stars, to smite proud Romans.
He courses with dread shout, he slays Rome's soldiers !
Through Caer Glew streets : who 'scaped his bloody
     glaive,
Leap in the fosse, from Britons' walls ; and perish !
   Might, lodged in leathern booths, Italic soldiers
Abide no longer, in an open field,
For the much rain. Then, under frozen ground,
Banked with green sods, they grave them Winter-
     bowers ;
Which trenched, they thatch, with river-reeds, above.

THE DAWN IN BRITAIN

Britons, within the town, one night-time, hear ;
Betwixt the flaws of wind, from further shore,
An Iscan voice, calling king Caradoc !
And saying ; that, to embark who sieged in
     Glevum,
Ride ready Kowain's ships, in Lower Hafren,
Returned from Erinn.   In those leaguered walls,
Silures now are nigh consumed by famine :
Nor left strike is of corn, in all the dune.
They every green thing, from the walls, have eaten,
Grass of their street, even dreary herb, which springs,
On new graves of the slain ; nor they might more
Endure.   One night, of weathers black and rough ;
Caradoc and Maglos gather ; and lead forth
The weary people armed, to river part ;
Whence issuing now, and without fear of Romans,
(Whose watch, cold-trembling, shroud them, in
     night-storm,)
Blue Britons, Hafren's floor, of stony frost,
Tread, which upbears them.   There, stout Maglos
     marched,
With a caterf, apart.   And those, to-night,
(Which have pitched tow wound, on their shafts and
     darts !)
Shall tempt, with shot, fire Romans' halm-thatcht camps.

THE DAWN IN BRITAIN

The remnant, following, with Caratacus,
Go crooked, in this cold.   Were those not passed
A mile ; when, looking back, they flames see rise,
To red skies, o'er their Roman enemies !
And joy the lean hearts, in their frozen breasts.
Yet, fainting, famisht, many, (in long night's murk,
Miswent,) fell in wide field, and naked wood ;
Wherethrough, hunt whining winds, and howl like
    wolves ;
Winds, which waft wings forth of some giant birds,
At the world's brinks !   The people and Caradoc,
(That bowed down, as with eld, in his fierce grief,
Like hird, before them goeth, upon his feet,)
Reach, when nigh is, at length, the day to break ;
Where they find Maglos, who arrived before,
At open strand, and Kowain's ready ships.
They kindle fires ; and sith, with Kowain's victual,
Being well refreshed, and there embarked the sick ;
Those march, these sail, to Caerwent ; to Moelmabon.

The next month, the proprætor overpassed,
To Gaul's mainland ; and journeys many days,
Towards Rome.   Being come now to the City
    Sovereign ;
And his relation, to the emperor Claudius,

Made ; he sent laureate letters, to the Senate ;
(Which sits, to hear them read, without the walls,
In temple of Bellona.)   The *Ovation*,
Then, common sentence of those conscript sires,
Decrees, to Cæsar's thrice victorious legate,
In the Britannic warfare, Aulus Plautius.
    He, myrtle-crowned, sith, with magnific pomp ;
And merry sound of flutes, and high-day shouts,
And solemn chant ; (lo, imperial Claudius walks,
Britannicus, at the left hand of Aulus !)
Upmounts, to temple-arx, of Rome's trine gods !

    But, absent Aulus, nations, late subdued,
Revolt.   Then all whom take crude Roman soldiers,
They kill.   And Geta caused, to be proclaimed,
Amongst the tribes, in Britain's Roman pale,
Briton, with whom found weapon, might be
    sold.
And may of any, in flight, (without re-
    course,)
Be slain.   Who hideth an enemy, in his
    house,
By forfeiture, should be punished, of his
    goods :
And, in what field is found a Roman slain ;

Three Britons shall be crucified, for the
    dead:
But, and the homicide were not known, three
    Britons
Being taken, by lot, of who next dwell, shall
    there
Those, for him, die. Given this third year of
    Claudius.

    Woe to a nation, when her dukes are fallen!
And word, concerning Beichiad, now, went forth,
Among the gods. He rector of war-chariots,
That seemed, in field, a bolt of thundering Taran,
May not long live. Broods pestilence, in the land,
As unquenched smouldering embers in an hearth.
    When, before Camulus' walls, were squadroned war-
    carts,
Put to the worse, and many overthrown;
Left fallen, in bloody field, at afternoon,
Was Beichiad, bleeding rife, from many wounds;
(Being, through the shoulder, stricken of a dart,)
Mongst broken carts; and buffeting their pierced
    steeds.
For none had marked, though he their duke, was hurt
Cunobelin's son, and his companion slain;

When scattered, in that plain, they scaped from death.
  Poor Briton wives, which night-time their dead
    sought,
In field, him found.   Of those, four, in their arms,
Took Beichiad up; and in some thicket hid;
Where he them showed, beside the lower Colne.
And sith, in wicker bark, past Hiradoc's cliffs,
Which look o'er East-main, towards free forest
    Almaigne,
Hurt Beichiad, closely, was conveyed : and rowed
The prince, some wounded East-men fugitives.

  Then Beichiad, one year's space, in Heligan's house,
Lay sick of his heart's sorrow, and strange disease :
(Heligan, unvanquished Coritavian prince,
His kinsman.)   Drew then unseen mortal shaft,
Of envious demon, Belisama forth,
From his pined corse ; and Camulus his wood rage,
In him, inspired.   And wains, which Beichiad sought,
Old Heligan gave, and victual, arms and chariot ;
And warriors' band, to march with him, in aid,
Of warlord Caradoc, who in far West March :
Now mid of Winter is, when these part forth.

  Their ways the frozen streams, for fear of Romans,
By night : they lurk, by day, in Winter woods.
But, on the hero, falls new languishment,

THE DAWN IN BRITAIN

When their shrill wheels, at length, passed over Avon.
Beichiad rends, lo, with furious hands, his harness ;
He gapes, with wildered front, for living breath !
With lean uplifted looks, now stares distract ;
Nor knows himself the prince, in this excess.
  His warriors halted, they consult ; To Caradoc,
The most then hold, march on.   Journeying the rest,
As he is able, who now sick to death ;
These bring him safely forth, towards forest place,
(In Dobuni March ;) where his milk-brethren wonne.

  Gainst dawn, arrive their creaking wheels, in glade,
Where cabans white with snow ; as in that wood,
Seems moonlight, all by day.   Stand weaponed men,
Come forth at door, for perilous is the time ;
To look on strange wain, driven to their poor lodge !
  But, whenas Beichiad those, their brother prince,
Know ; and hear tiding of his strange disease :
They gaze, on him, amazed ; and mourn their hearts !
In their strong arms, with manly derne lament ;
They bear him in, as one lies nigh to death.
No ignoble fear them turns, from him, away.
  He wakes !   They kiss death, on his clay-cold lips ;
And his clam front, his hands, his knees, they kiss.
Is this the pestilence ; they would, (say their hearts,)

THE DAWN IN BRITAIN

Decease in the self manner of his death!
On hazel sprays, deckt with ox-hide, for bed;
They him, the best in that poor place, have laid.
The old milk-father kneeling, by his prince,
Kindles much fire; and aye he weeps, and weep
All those poor wights, that live by daily sweat;
With burning drops, as manly hearts can weep.
They still, on Beichiad, gaze; who lies past speech.
And look, upon them all, aye his dull eyes;
As who would say, Farewell!   His woodman's hands,
Gently, in murmuring some, his, magic, spell;
That foster, on his nourseling's dying breast,
Lays: dreads, his prince's flickering pulse doth cease!
Ah, now is, ceased! (and fades, with kindly warmth,)
The vital breath, for ever, from his lips.
Rose loud, then, lamentable voice of sobs;
Of fosters of the dead, and his wain-servants:
But cannot wake the corse, when it is cold!
The man's sons, sith, with axes, wend for wood;
To strew the pyre, beside their mother's grave.
When midday past, and this full-ended was;
Ah! all suddenly, who the elder, smote himself,
Riving his gorge; and fell down gurgling blood,
Upon the funeral wood.   Nor would he Beichiad;
That both had suckt one mother's breast, survive.

THE DAWN IN BRITAIN

Then brother, brother's body ; in night of grief,
Much weeping, drew apart, and sprent with snow ;
Lest their sire, finding, should himself fordo.
So, with a frozen heart, this turned his steps :
(Ah, heavy day, ah, heavy house, of death !)
To get him home.   The sire, behold, comes forth,
From threshold of their lodge.   That father asks,
With trembling voice, why he returns alone ?
What purple stain, this on his woodman's weed ?
(His brother's blood, as he the dying kissed !)
Father, is whortleberries' juice, he saith.
Nay, in Winter, ben none whortleberries ;
    where,
Quoth he, where is, thy brother ; where, my son ?
He waits us, father, at the mother's tomb !
   Entered the cattle-byre, they find one dead,
Of East-men drivers, come with Beichiad's wain.
Another sick lies, in their bower, to death,
Of the self ill.   The father sickens soon ;
Grows cold.   He, laid by Beichiad, his dead son,
Him down ; departed, at mid-afternoon.
   Two drivers rest, beside the foster's son :
And these all have ado, bear the dead forth ;
Wain-lay, the beasts yoke, and to pyreward drive ;
Feeling now inward ill, on themselves, seize.

They by their brother prince, that brother laid ;
And, in the midst, their sire, built broad the
    wood :
And Beichiad's servants at his head and feet.
Each lifting faithful hands then, to their gods,
To other, swears, to lay him on the pyre ;
Who shall survive, when goeth this sun beneath ;
And kindle funeral flame, under the dead.

Now eve ; and turns, in twilight, from Caerwent ;
Whither the foster sent him, (when his sons
Were come again, from the woadstained caterfs,
With Maglos and warlord Caratacus,)
Their thrall.   But he, arrived, finds empty house ;
Nor burning hearth, nor beasts, nor any wight.
Sith following, in the moonshine, their wheels' trace,
He his household finds, with strangers dead, pyre-laid !
And who last died, was fallen forth on the wood.
Is Beichiad he perceives, who midst them lies ;
Well-known, unto the thrall, his noble face,
So like king Caradoc.   Loud, he mourns ; nor wots
How all his, thus, not battle-slain, lie dead !
None, save their old house-hound, that howling wards
The sacred corses, yet, is left alive ;
And oxen of the plough, with drooping heads.

That thrall, long marvelling, in the bleak moonlight,
Stood sighing : last he spark of flint-flake, strake ;
Blew, cherished, twixt his palms, the kindling flame ;
Which, crackling, with much smoke, to frosty stars,
Ascends.   So hardly he, in frozen ground,
Digged, and this night-time, opened hasty grave ;
Wherein, at day, with sighs, their cindered bones
He laid.   He stayed not enter in the house ;
But took his way, all weary as he was.
By forest, wild, he went back, and he ran ;
And repassed Hafren, came to Deheubarth,
And showed king Caradoc his brother's death !

BOOK XIX

ARGUMENT

Aulus builds strongholds in the East Marches. Kowain, sailing with Duneda's ships, harries the lands of traitorous Bericos and Cogidubnos. Death of king Bericos. Caradoc, Summer ended, returns to Moelmabon. Almain strangers arrive, in mourning weed. After meat, they declare; that Thorolf is fallen, in battle! Dark grief of Briton kings and warriors. Wittig's messengers have brought gifts of ornaments and arms. They tell of that great battle, wherein Thorolf fell; and of his high funerals.

Caratacus encumbered with grief, goes forth to the starry Night; but miswent, in his path, he is come now to the grave-field. There, in his frenzy, he would have slain himself: but a vision withholds him of his germain, Togodumnos. With sword of Thorolf, (which was of Brennus,) Caratacus slays the rinded trees! Belisama, shining goddess, descends from heaven. She watches over the hero's sleep. Wakens the king, at dawn; and now come unto himself, Caradoc returns home.

Another Spring-time is in; and Kowain, sailed forth, destroys Roman ships. He is wind-driven thence to Aban, fair Brigantine haven. Kowain returning through the sea of Severn, is cast over, by storm, unto Erinn; where he comes to his king Duneda.

Tumult of Iceni grows in Roman East Province. Ostorius' horse are gulfed in Meltraith Fleets. Caratacus, carried, by the fury of his steed to a *castrum* gate, is saved by his god Camulus.

Then war is renewed in Britain. Ostorius, Cæsar's new legate, succeeds to Aulus. Night-battle in a forest. Britons assail the marching Romans, which have that day the worse. Upon the morrow, when battle is renewed, Titus and king Caratacus fight.

The warlord journeying, mongst Britons' Northern tribes, is in danger to be felonously cut-off in his sleep. Duneda's navy is burned in Severn. East-men choose now Cathigern their duke. Ostorius, marching through Mid-Britain; receives, from Cartismandua, a secret embassage.

Out of the West, ascends Caratacus. Ostorius marches to meet him. The legate's oration to his soldiers. War-sacrifice of druids. King Caradoc's last speech to blue Britons.

BOOK XIX

Being nigh the time, when should, in Britain, Aulus
Lay down his charge ; the legate cast, how best
He might leave peaceable, this warlike Province ;
And have, in Rome, therefore, a thank of Cæsar.
To which end now, twixt Avon and the Ouse,
He fortify will all river-passages.

He sends one Sylvius, captain of fleet-soldiers,
From Camulodunum, through Icenic marches,
To build strongholds ; and chiefly a great square burgh,[1]
Measured of lime and stone, like legions' *castra*,
In field ; wherein, fast by the flood of Yare,
Might garrison lodge, gainst inroads from the North,
Of Britons yet untamed ; and delve beneath,
(Station for longships, gainst the Saxon pirates,)
An hythe ; and fence with banks and battled towers.

But when is Sylvius, thither, now arrived ;
He, to those servile tasks, conscribes free Britons !
Men namely Iceni, which of Bericos' part ;

[1] Now called Burgh Castle.

Had promised only, to yield Cæsar tribute,
Not vanquished were. Perceive those then ; would
    Romans
Lay a perpetual yoke of servitude,
Under that name of lordship, on their march.

   Sails, in first moon of the returning year,
From sea of Severn, with Duneda's navy,
(Wherein sit thousand chosen warriors ;)
Young valorous Kowain. Come then morning red,
Of the eighth day ; now entering in Colne mouth,
Their long war-keels, Dumnonians row to land :
Whence hastily gone up, bands of glittering spears ;
Fair Mersea isle those waste, and homesteads burn ;
And, therein, every stranger woman-born,
Whomso they meet, slay ; be he Gaul or Roman.
Some taken alive, (already dead for fear ;)
They hanged, as public robbers, in green trees.
Smoke of that sea-road was, from their new walls,
Seen of the Claudian Colony, in Camulodunum !
   But lifting anchors, ere pursuit arrived,
Of Gaulish horse ; those hoised to merry wind,
Broad sails, plough forth, Dumnonian twelve war-keels,
Heavy with spoils of Romans. Fallen that night,
They made again the land, furl in Stour Frith.

THE DAWN IN BRITAIN

At dawn, to make his name the more abhorred,
They steads burn of the people of Bericos;
And seeded fields o'errun, from shore, and waste.
But veering soon the wind, embarked Dumnonians,
Invoked their blue sea-gods, steer South, longs strand.
Next even, they sailing, under island Vectis,
Unlooked-for, in white moonshine, row to land;
And Belges' field burn, subject now to Romans.
There, having reaved much corn, they lade their ships.

Was, in these Summer days, cursed of all Britons,
Forsaken of all góds, fell Bericos
Deceased; prince which had Britain's Isle betrayed:
For Bericos, Claudius Cæsar, purpled sot,
First moved, in Rome, Britannia to invade.
That flatterer and Cæsarian royal Briton;
Riding with train of clients of his house,
(Men which were, mostwhat, bounden in his debt,)
Full of old wine and surfeit of strange Romans;
An over-fat lord, in the Summer's heat,
From hallowing Claudius' fane at Camulodunum;
Belin, the Sun-god, smote his treacherous pate;
His Briton steed him cast then, in waste heath;
And bandied back again, that foster earth,
(Which seemed, bewrayed, recuse,) his recreant corse.

THE DAWN IN BRITAIN

Icenians fall then, from oppressing Romans ;
Whose tumult, that *Colonia nova* of Claudius,
Threatens : whereto arrived, the legate Aulus
Summons before him, lords of all East March ;
Unto whom, reciting merits of the Romans ;
He wills they, in room of deceased Bericos,
Receive, for king, his uncle Prasutagos.

This saying, the legate bound, in Cæsar's name,
That prince's brows, with royal diadem.
And being a great rich lord this Prasutagos,
In cattle and land and goods and gold and thralls ;
And one that ever gave his voice for Romans ;
He trusts thus void occasion of new stirs.

These things determined, Thames again passed
    Aulus ;
And, three days, Westward rides, to Cogidubnos :
Whose Rome-built city, Regnum,[1] gins, lo, rise,
Under white windy hills ; whence, to sea-waves,
Through wide champaign, ship-bearing stream down-
    flows.

Lo, on the morrow, amidst their market-place,
On judgment seat, sits the proprætor Aulus ;
And purpled Cogidubnos, (who Tiberius,
Claudius, now named, in Roman wise ; and styled

---

[1] Chichester.

For Cæsar's business, mongst the Belges Britons,
Imperial Legate,) sits at his right hand ;
Being girt, his brows, with royal diadem !
  Then certain, noted in the late revolt,
Britons, led, gyved, before the Roman duke ;
Conscious of guilt, embrace his knees ! whom
    Aulus
Pardons : but who convinced of crimes, he judged,
Some, to be sold ; a few damned of their heads :
Other, reputed turbulent, hath commanded
The legate, to be beaten with green rods.
  Departing thence, now all his horse sends Aulus ;
To seek, eachwhere, and they Caratacus
Might take.   But found, no Briton, in these wars,
Is, that betray, for torment, or for meed,
Would Caradoc's lurking place.   What glory had
    Aulus ;
And he might lead that hero, in chains, to Rome !
  Standing on scaffolds and all temple-roofs,
Should Romans, longs the Sacred Way, applaud ;
To see, pass Britons' king by, to his death :
Aye, and him acclaim ; and they should likely name
Him, colleague-consul, with the emperor Claudius ;
When, next year, he should have returned from
    Britain.

THE DAWN IN BRITAIN

Another Summer season is now ended ;
And dukes, to Winter *castra*, fenced with banks,
And towers, withdraw, from field, again, their
    legions.
Caradoc, with Maglos, leading blue caterfs,
Returns through Deheubarth, to Moelmabon.
Where come, in one high-settle, silent sits,
(Devising aye destruction of strange Romans,)
King Caradoc, daylong, with Silures' sire.
Over against them, Maglos sits, with Kynan ;
In equal see, mongst captains, lords, and druids.
  Winter is in, when twilight all by day :
Nor cure men drink of *curmi*, or sweet mead ;
Nor any list, so darkened is their cheer,
Such heaviness in all hearts, hear evening tales.
And idle hangs the crowth, whose chords no
    more,
His hands may wake, who perished in the war.
  Sit silent on, amazed, those Caerwent lords,
Oft casting down their eyeballs, to the fire ;
Whilst dumb is every wonted cheerful sound :
Only his purblind soaring looks, uplifts
Moelmabon, oftwhiles, to his battle-gods !
Uneasy, in settle, sits Caratacus ;
Whose high heart aches, within his straitened chest !

THE DAWN IN BRITAIN

Come strangers in, lo, from the gable-porch!
Towards the high seat they pass before the hearths!
Four men, whose raiment both and bearded looks,
And arms, do show them plainly to be Almains.
Wayfarers, those arrive, in mourning sort:
For blackened be their hose and wadmel coats,
And ash-strewn, their polled heads and visages.
    These ridden have, day and night, from their long-
        yawls,
At East sea-cliff; to king Caratacus.
Nay, and some those messengers had, erewhile, at
        Verulam
Seen, helm-clad, harnessed, leading Thorolf's spears;
For are they lords, which come from Wittig's march.
The strangers sit down, mongst king's Winter-
        guests;
But none spake word, in hall of Moelmabon!
    Britons do whisper, lords still on them gaze;
Expecting those should speak; yet none asks tiding,
Till the king's guests have eaten. In deep-lipped
        horns,
Bears Darfran, steward, them sweet-breathed methe-
        glin:
And Almains, silent, drinking out, salute
The Briton kings. Anon, are tables set,

Before the strangers ; whereon wheaten loaves,
And brawn of tuskéd swine : but when those Almains
Now ended have to sup ; What tiding, asks
Moelmabon, they, from over-seas, him-brought?
    With slow and husking voice, of them that mourn ;
Those answer to Moelmabon, make again,
Such as they couth, in halting Briton tongue ;
Thorolf is fallen, in battle, and ship-laid!
    When heard this grievous word, as endless night
Of death, on soul sinks of Caratacus!
Who mantle drew, much labouring his vast chest,
O'er his stern altered face.   Loved the war-sire
That Elbe-land ethling ; and had Thorolf's power,
In Britain, countervailed a Roman legion !
    Groans Moelmabon, king of warlike men.
He old, in that remembering his sons' deaths,
Commiserates Wittig ; left, midst foes, alone,
Without sustain, in warlike land of Almaigne.
    Sounds, in king's hall, confused constraint of men :
For stricken of enemy's dart him-seems each one.
Then brast, in loud lament, the strangers forth.
Seem Winter eaves, of melting icicles !
Those Almains' cragged brows.   Rose voice mongst
    Britons,
Of manly plaint ; as each, of fallen kin,

Records, in war with Rome: nor Thorolf few,
In Britain, had, in battle, saved from death!
  The people, when even is come, gin now depart
Forth, one by one, to sup.   When only rest
Kings, lords and druids, with their Almaigne guests,
The sire's mead-hall is shut.   Then Fredigern,
Cousin to Wittig, noblest of these strangers,
Lo, opens gifts.   This ale-horn, silver-lipped,
(Of ureox, which had, when he came to Almaigne,
For love of Fridia, hand slain of great Brennus,)
They bring, for a remembrance, to Moelmabon.
  This Thorolf's collar, cunning handiwork,
Of Weyland, of the fine burned gold embossed,
An hunt shows of grey wolves; and this, (which
      was
The homicide brand of great Rome-conquering Bren-
      nus ;)
Wherewith slew thousand, his resistless hand ;
And fed the wolves, in Britain and Mainland,
To his great kinsman, king Caratacus,
King Wittig sends.   This raven-helm, of bronze,
And Thunor's golden hammer ornament;
Which hanged, from Thorolf's nape, on his vast
      chest :
And this the hero's brooch, of a palm's breadth ;

Bright jewel, which like golden sun is wrought;
To his son's battle-fellows, generous sons
Of Moelmabon, Wittig, father, sends.

When   lords   have   mourned, and   noble   women
        wept,
In hall, their fill; desiring him that dead
Is, whiles, with sighs, men name the hero oft;
One Radwald, mongst the Almains, gan rehearse;
(Left sick, in Thorolf's ships, had Radwald seen
That field;) how fighting gainst great armed inroad,
Fell Thorolf.   Gathered to him hastily were,
From Elbe-land's borders, (home of warriors,)
Stout men, not many, which returned from Britain.
With riders, and with bowmen, Getas were
Great army.   Thorolf then, all day, their charge
Sustained.   Rattled loud dints, on shields, of spears
And swords; and oft seemed dimmed heaven and the
        world;
With the infinite many of shafts, which Getas shot.
    Round the   ethling, foremost   champions   fell, till
        eve :
In tempest bursten was of Getas' spears,
His white-horse shield; his iron war-kirtle hanged,
Bloody, on his panting chest, to-hewed, to-rent.

Gold-bristles, then, the hero cast, to ground,
(His helm); so dasht, so hackt to shards, it was.
  His enemies fled, when rang it on the stones,
Aback, aghast! Then seeing impossible thing,
Were scape this field; sith might not he, alone,
Contend, with thousand flocking enemies, champions:
Disdaining come, in Getas' hands, alive;
Calling aloud on Woden, his sires' Sire,
He leapt, midst thicket of strong Getas' spears;
And hewed him round, all-weary, as he was;
A bay of death. Then Thorolf's furious hand,
Point turned of spear, (which now he broken hath;)
Turned in against himself! and his great force,
Through-smote, neath his rent hauberk, his ribbed
    chest!
  Like to some root-fast pine, which gods, of storm,
At length o'erthrow, that ruins, in vast space,
Fell Thorolf forth! Sith, o'er his bleeding corse,
Fell, till the last one, Thorolf's lords and champions.
  But the same night his foes, which held that field,
Rendered great Thorolf, with his arms and harness!
Drawn forth, from bloody bank of mingled slain;
They sent his body, on bier of ashen green;
With heralds, granting pause of hostile arms,
In worship of the illustrious hero dead.

THE DAWN IN BRITAIN

And was, when gathered spoil, at morrow's eve ;
And buried now all weapon-slain, in field,
Bearing pine-boughs, with blackened visages,
In shining harness, Getas' princely men
Marched, men of stature, and many have war-
    wounds ;
To Saxen Thorolf's solemn funerals.
    Nigh was that field of fight, to creeky haven ;
On whose shole strand, lay Thorolf's snake-necked
    ships ;
And the king's dragon-keel, with gilded ensigns ;
Hight the Goldorm.   There, after day's lament,
Of Thorolf's sea-folk ; and few left of his,
'Scaped from that field, to ship ; four enemy dukes,
And Catlif, (who the king of Getas' son,)
Convey great Brennid Thorolf, washed from blood,
Fair as in life, on his white battle-steed,
(Freyfax, borne in his ship,) upstayed to ride.
    Men of his keels, lift reverent down the dead ;
And bear, slow-paced, on Catlif's door-like targe,
With mourning hearts, over salt strand, aboard
Goldorm ; where, on high stool of polished elm,
Rune-graven, and dight with plates 'of shining
    brass,
They stay him up, on pillows.   His dead brows,

Men crown with helm of antique Arthemail ;
(Gift, which once Tuscan Arunt sent to Brennus.)
They laid his bruised targe, of the linden, light,
Dight with hard hairy hide of the ureox ;
(Gift of Hild, Elsing, who his foster, was ;)
That glorious gleamed, with whorles of tin and brass,
Covering the hero cold, on his large breast.
His peers, (dead ethlings and companion warriors ;)
Whose corses, in slow ox-wains, follow his,
Men lay him round, all on the rowers' banks.
Last Briton hounds, and his slain battle-steed ;
To burn with him, in the two stems, they laid.
His own then, and all truth-plight Geta men,
Great plenty of darts and shafts, which gathered were,
In slaughter field, heap round those Woden-dead :
So that was seen, like hoy, high-fraught, with wood,
Of Goldorm, soon, the royal warlike board.
Then sea-folk smeared, the funeral ship, with pitch ;
And cast in tallow and fat.   Sit friends, sit foes,
Kindled great fires, with torches in their hands ;
Waiting the cresset moon, when he should rise !
Lightens, before his coming, now wide East.
Gin shipswains, knees, from under Goldorm's bilge,
Withdraw and shoring-staves : climbed some, aboard,
Large mainsail hoise ; and loose out to night wind.

THE DAWN IN BRITAIN

Cast noble Getas gifts ; saies storied bright,
With needlework ; proud arms, into the ship,
Vessail and ornaments ; to great Thorolf's spirit !
   In that, heard trampling hooves, and shimmering
     seen :
(Is dread, by night-time, sudden gleam of bronze !)
Getas, round shields embraced, grip long war-spears :
They, truce-plight foes, that funeral keel close round ;
Ready, and need wére, to fight, till their own deaths,
Tall men of war, to ward great Thorolf's corse.
   Heard lamentable women's shrieks, anon !
From steed, all of a foam, Elfrida, eftsoon,
Alights ; true wife of that great hero dead :
And, ere-year, were their joyous spousals made !
With her rides an armed company ; and, lo, old Gizla,
Mourning milk-mother of the ethling Thorolf.
   Warned them prophetic virgin, Veleda, crying,
Yester, from tower-head, in the wind ; she saw
Great Thorolf's ghost, received amongst the
     gods !
Haste men to sea-strand ; where they, yet,
     should find
His body slain, mongst oath-plight enemies.
   With few, they hied then, hither ; on swift steeds ;
Nor stinted, day-time, nor night-long, to ride ;

Abstaining from all kindly nourishment.
Last heard they, of some wayfaring man, this
    eve;
Where lay that death-field, fast by the salt waves;
And Thorolf dead, mongst soothfast enemies!
  Those noble ladies; in whom life and breath
Remains, uneath, Getas lift on the ship.
Shrieks Elfrida, beholding, under stars,
How her dead Thorolf sits, a solemn corse,
Among the dead. She, passing to him, swoons.
But Gizla, kissed the lord, son of her paps,
From head to foot, fell down, at Thorolf's knees;
And there lay still, in cloud of death; for brast,
The weary heart, within her feeble breast.
  The queen reviving, in the evening wind;
When Gizla she beheld already passed!
Disdaining any her, to her dead love,
Prevent, in cragged path, of Hel, swart goddess,
Uprose; and embraced Thorolf's shielded corse;
Her white hand, ere there any might withhold;
Snatcht spear-head, of those heaped from slaughter-
    place,
Wherein he fell, she launcht her widow's breast!
And sinks Elfrida, bleeding, on them both.
  Great sigh went up, from all that mourning folk!

THE DAWN IN BRITAIN

And she, nigh-spent, makes sign, with dying hand !
On whose white wrist, shines long-wreathed golden
    bracelet ;
And, from her bright brow, as she beckoned, sliding
Her rochet, that is hemmed with precious ermine ;
The fainting lily-fair young queen is seen,
Gold-dight.   Upon her front, moon-sheen broad fret,
Of far-fetcht pearls ; and hangs, like Brisings-men,[1]
Of sea-stones, dew-drop clear, a shining lace,
Down from her gracious neck : (will Chaucan's queen,
Elfrida, her spousal ornaments bring again,
To Thorolf, even in hell !) Sign, makes she then ;
Put fire, launch out! Priests hallow Thorolf's
    corse
With the hammer of high Thunor god : sith all
Those corses dead ; and they her dying bless !
Many together heaving, then, thrust forth,
From shore, the funeral ship, down to salt deep !

    Like swan, which proudly breasts the tide, her yards
Belayed and rudder-bands, Goldorm now sails
Forth, on night frith, where lightly blows the wind.
All cry, Farewell! which watch on the sea-strand.
    With wake of burning light, long drives the ship :

---

[1] A. Sax. *Brosinga-mene* (*monile*) ; the necklace of Freyja.

THE DAWN IN BRITAIN

And still men watch upon the sand ; and chant,
To Balder's hall, who fairest mongst the
   sons
Of Woden, named, is Thorolf's fiery voyage !
Till morning star, when now, like fisher's brand,
That funeral keel, which sithen seen no more.
Thorolf returned, (all cry then,) to the gods !
   A sennight long, cast friends, cast Getas, foes,
Then funeral mound, on foreland of that shore ;
Which shall, from age, (well-seen of all that sail,)
To age, to keep great Saxmund's name, endure.

   The bereaved fatherhood of Moelmabon,
Of Wittig asked ; and quaked the old king's voice ;
For like now both those sires, in endless loss !
   They tell how Wittig, to a sea-isle passed ;
And thence his royal words bare Higelac forth ;
Higelac, who, of all men of Almain speech,
For his well-shaping tongue, accepted is,
Next after Heorrenda,[1] the old, lay-smith ;
A wight divine : of whom, whilst dwelled, is told,
He yet mongst men, son of a king ; (yet some
Him, son of Bragi name, the maker-god ;

[1] Teutonic hero of song and glee-craft. A. Sax. *Heorrenda* ; Icel.
Hiarrandi.

THE DAWN IN BRITAIN

Ere took him, in their glittering hall, to sing,
In Asgarth, children of blithe blessed gods,)
What time he sate, to make, alone, in glade ;
Gathered to him all beasts, of field and wood,
All creeping things in grass ; worms under clod ;
Fowls, lighting to him, folded their swift wings ;
Sate on his shoulders, and his sacred knees :
Fishes left swimming, in the hasting stream ;
Which stayed, the while, and fell her roaring waves!
    Higelac then speeding, to Cheruscan kings,
From hall to hall ; invoked the Saxen gods !
Quoth lay, which he, of Thorolf's death, had made :
Him likens he, to Balder ; for whose death,
Wept all thing in mid-earth. Him, sighing, trees
Bewailed ; winds howled, and sweated rocks and
      stones ;
Stood speechless-beasts, in long astonishment !
Wights mourned and sprites ; and cast-down were the
      gods !
    Higelac sate, suppliant, at their Winter-hearths.
Then rose five Brennid kings, in furious mood ;
Which Woden breathéd, in their warlike breasts.
They sware, with enemies, men, and hostile gods,
Do battle, till world's doom, and their own deaths !
    Each levied a strong power, in his own mark ;

And come together, to moot-place, they choose
Great Awehelm, Friedemund's father, their proud
    duke :
Then marched those unto war.   And followed flocks
Of hoodie crows, ravens and howling wolves,
Their folkings forth.   Then Saxen kings thrice smote
The giant Getas : all his foes they strewed,
(Shouting dead Thorolf's name !) in Wittig's march.
Fell Catlif, slain, amongst the birds of death !
Honoured him Saxen heroes, with high mound.

  In sacred silence of night-stars, pale druids ;
From Moelmabon's hall, have made, gone forth,
Response: Lives, kinsman of Isle Britain's kings,
Thorolf, henceforth, in the divine abodes !
  Moelmabon, long-aged, purblind sire, then rose ;
And bowed him reverent, towards South part ; (from
    whence,
Men deemed, descend, into the world, the gods :)
And the remembrance-bowl, his trembling hand,
From Nessa, the hoar-headed queen, receiving,
(Ah, war-bereaved, with him, of generous sons !)
Wherein, and secretly, now some drowsy herbs
She steepéd hath ; (whereof, is faith, who tastes,
Should presently even forget a mother's death !)

THE DAWN IN BRITAIN

First, on the floor, he pours, before the gods,
Out golden mead, to their dread powers, beneath ;
So tastes: then tastes the warsire Caradoc ;
Kynan sith, the sire's sons, and warlike peers.
Thorolf! all standing, call with moaning voice!

Descended, from high settle, Caradoc,
Nor salutes any ; and to high night, went forth.
The king's doorward, his lean infested looks,
Marked ; fixt his austere gaze, on the cold loft ;
Where, after daily funerals of the sun,
Shine stars' caterfs, that silent rise and pass ;
(Wherein, of men, that Belt-of-strength is seen,
Of heavenly gods !) as he there sought dead Thorolf.
In Caradoc's hand, gleams Marvor, that lean blade ;
Which, in old days of Brennus, vanquished Rome.
The warlord treads forth, on white Winter-mould,
Of snow : and Caradoc still afflicts himself ;
Nor ceases, with his deadly heart, commune.
Him-seems, in every bush, meet Thorolf's ghost !
Had entered Caradoc path, to Embla's house ;
But travailing much, in busy troubled thought ;
At parting of two ways, oblivious ;
So clouds of sorrow cumber and oppress ·
His sense, the sire miswent; or demons, else,

THE DAWN IN BRITAIN

Misled, of ground or wood.   Was mid of night ;
When looked he, see now his own lighted porch,
Under hill side ; behold is the corpse-field !
Where, men of Caerwent, fallen, in war with Rome,
Lie in grave-mould : this place is known to him.
    He oft himself, with warriors, lords and druids,
Came hither, following wailful funerals ;
(And orphans' outcries heard, and widows' shrieks !)
He saw men borne forth, dead of Roman wounds,
Upon their pictured shields.   Moelmabon's sons,
Ferriog and Merion, hither were conveyed,
In welted hides of bulls, from far in Britain ;
Bounden their corses were on blackened steeds :
And lie those graved now, under frozen snow ;
Yonder, in shadow of the royal mound,
In this bleak moonshine.   And who slain, and burned,
In their war-weed, on many an high-strewed pyre
Silures' chief ones, their white cindered bones,
Uplaid in honey and fat, sent hither were.
And pight, at each mound's head, is some wild stone,
Wherein scored token seen ; that men, which knew
His shield in warlike field, his name might read,
Who lies, (cast carcase, clay, neath clay !) beneath.
    The sire records then, one by one, their names ;
Their fellowship in high hall, their hardy deeds.

THE DAWN IN BRITAIN

On these dead silent warriors, Winter lies ;
Whose lodging was the iron wall of their harness :
Whose memory, and their high praise, from living
    breasts :
Doth fade like passing sound, of trampling steeds !
   The warsire sate him down, at a grave's head ;
And glory, embraced that mounded foster-earth,
(Whose sacred Womb her children doth receive,
Again,) to his dead battle-fellows, gave
Caratacus.   He calls young Ketternac,
To mind, who sleeps here, fathom-deep beneath,
A buried corse. Life of that noble youth,
He himself, in Camulodunum field, had saved :
At Caer Glew, sith, young Ketternac was pierced ;
Tempting, with Maglos, burn the Roman work.
   Hurt unto death, of his kinsfolk, borne forth
On wattled boughs, to ship ; he lived yet pass
The threshold of great hall of Moelmabon :
And heard the loved youth bard touch harp, and chant
His hardy deeds. The mead-bowl at his lips,
He pledged Caratacus, and yielded breath !
   The warsire dasht a woman's tear, (that wells,
Unwares, for man is woman-born,) aside !
And gazing on these burials of dead warriors'
Flesh ; (now new guests, all they, in Hall of Death !)

THE DAWN IN BRITAIN

Of whom not few fell him beside ; gan muse
The warlord's heavy heart ; where have their being,
Beneath, or in what circuit of yond stars,
Disbodied souls ! and what is that which saith
An antique funeral chant of Verulam druids ?
Spent spirits, rekindled, at the Light, above,
Revert, from stars, to be new bodies' guests :
And other hymn, Are men the living dead !
　　But who lie, gaping upright, in the grave,
Whose rottenness we rue ; ben not their deaths,
(Night-sleep, this iron griesly grip, which hath
None wakening, clod laid under clodded earth,)
Surcease of burdens, and of every pain,
Less grievous than our life, which yet, the sun
See'th ; that, like sháft's flight, tossed in every blast ;
Whereon, again, the woundless air doth close :
Or like as tainted footstep, in this snow,
Soon fading ; which, therewith, doth utterly perish !
But, and when cometh aught thing, of good, to us,
Is that a seldom grace !　King Caradoc felt
His heart, like burning coal, in his cold breast,
For Thorolf's death, his brother, in Mainland.
　　Where were ye then, O gods?　Were warlike arms
To his conjoined, of unsubduéd Almaigne ;
Should not, together, they have vanquished Rome !

THE DAWN IN BRITAIN

When he bethinks him, son of dead Cunobelin,
Then, of his germain, martial Togodumnos,
Morag and Golam, Ferriog and Bodvocos,
Brentyn and Fythiol, and Heroidel slain,
With many more ; and now lord Beichiad dead,
New fiery torment kindles all his being.
He snow, with his two hands, whelms on his head !
 Him-seemeth now left, alone, in a dead world,
Mongst these unbound. Such, on his weary spirit,
Then darkness falls, him-thought, ceased heavenly stars,
To shine above : and sighed Caratacus ;
We perish, praying to insensate gods !
Are men ungodly? ben not yé, O proud gods,
Inhuman ! or have ye no power to save?
(When gods, their faces, turn away from us ;
Must not mishappen thing we undertake ;
That, groping, few life-days, still wrestling
  pass !)
 Ye careless stars, which shine, in chambered
  night,
Shield-hall of heaven, like cierges clear ; whereon
Hang fates of men ; and ye indeed be gods,
Rid us of Roman strange invading enemies !
 Him-seemed, then, his own soul, in waking vision,

THE DAWN IN BRITAIN

In likeness see of caged small writhing vivern,
(The cognizance of great Cunobelin's house,)
And peeping gods, gigantic visages,
Which balefires, mocking, kindle him around.
    He rose then up, as one that wakes in dream
Of sorrow, and so stood still.   On his brainpan,
Him-seems sink deadly whelming weight ; as some
Giant hélm were, which, so sore, him doth oppress.
He sweats, part Caradoc trembles, in the cold !
Him burns dire thought, in breast, sharp tooth, short
        stroke,
Even of this antique blade, should lay to rest,
His life, which now forsaken of his gods :
One pang end all ! like unto his, who leaps
In chilling wave : so loost all cares, to-night ;
Should sleep, lifted, for ever, from his breast,
This raging smart ; and passed his soul from earth,
Descend unto the fathers' forepast spirits.
    He is alone, with Death, in this dark wood ;
And, with a frozen heart, that homicide hand
Of Caradoc feels, among the mounded dead,
The mouth adown, of lean devouring blade ;
Whereon, fame is, had perished Second Brennus !
Less dread, him-thinks, that griesly face of death,
Than this disease of life, which is ; whereas,

THE DAWN IN BRITAIN

He, as from sea's cliff, sees none further path.
  In that last desolation of his spirit,
Him-seems, stoop, semblant, from white moon-rid
    cloud,
Of his great germain, buried Togodumnos ;
Draws back his hand !   Thou great upholding spirit,
Dost, in his fatal hour, thy germain save !
  Abasht, wox Caradoc ; and there fell new thought,
As from the gods, in his heroic breast ;
What joy should, to his enemies ! be his death,
Grief to all Britons ! left, without sustain,
Ah, Embla and their sweet babe : were vanquished, then,
Blue tribes' resistance, in this Roman war ;
Should not they be, ah, captives, sent to Rome,
To deck a triumph : through Rome's city led ;
Of some foul gaoler, ah ! outraged in their chains,
Sith strangled ! last hurled from that bloody stair ;
Whence, of the common hangman, drawn with hooks,
Their royal flesh be cast, as enemies' corses,
In flood of Tiber !   Caradoc, again, thrust
That baleful brand down in his sheath ! and took
Cunobelin's warlike son, anew, his breath.
  Soughs the night-wind ; and smite with dreary
    sound,
The forest boughs together : but that spirit

THE DAWN IN BRITAIN

His godlike front allays.   Rose the warsire,
And he mounts forth.   His soul longs thither, where,
He might, with wolves, howl, bell with the grave-owl ;
And bellow forth the woodness of his soul !
Nor come unto men's living ears, his voice.
  And, is it the wild hunt, in skies, he hears ?
Furious night-host ; wherein fell Morrigu rides,
And her swart hags, with hounds of fiery breath.
The Guledig's cry, him-seems, that fares in clouds,
And Antethrigus' shout, which rings above !
That headless hunter drives, in heaven's wide heath.
  It is, in the night woods, wolves' murderous voice ;
Which glutted, ere, in slaughter-fields, their gulfs ;
Wherein fell flower, of Britons' comely youth :
But deems them Caradoc, in his wildered mood,
Romans, werewolves, and their wolf-suckled kings !
Through glade, with gait of giant, the hero fares.
Would, mongst these wind-cast beams, his strong
      fierce hands
Their crude abhorred hearts, rent up, by the roots !

  Issued, like lamp, from wild wood of the skies,
Now moon outshines ; and cast great forest stems,
Whose crooked boughs rock on this frozen wind,
Swart shadows ; and weep oft their snowy crests,

THE DAWN IN BRITAIN

Down on sheen hulver thicket boughs, beneath.
Caradoc them deems, who now, night-dreamer walks,
With   darkened   mood,   shafts,   harnessed   Roman
    soldiers :
And wind-gusts, piping loud, blow like an horn !
    Like ureox, then, he rushed ; and rang dark forest,
With battle-shout of great Caratacus !
With that Rome-quelling brand, which ere of Brennus,
He slays, (alas, for ruth !) the rinded trees.
Romans him-thought those stedfast timber-ranks ;
Him-seemed his hands smote tribunes and centurions.
    Last stumbling Caradoc forth, on   some   gnarled
    root ;
(So that strong vertue, of drowsy herbs, now wrought ;
Which Nessa steeped, in hall, in the king's mead ;)
Wallowed in snow, the warsire slumbers fast.
Rest hero, sleep, under these starry gods !
    Like to some swart vast fowl, how silent Night,
(As Day she covered, with her dusky wings,)
Broods o'er dim sullen round, of earth and woods !
It night of the moon-measurer of the year,
Is, wherein Belisama, eyebright goddess,
Girded in kirtle blue, with woodwives sheen,
Wont to fare forth ; and her shield-maidens' train,
And loud hounds, in the forest-skies above.

THE DAWN IN BRITAIN

She, Caradoc seeing, stays her aery wain :
And, marvelling! in cloud-cliff, her divine team
She bound : so lights this faery queen, benign,
(Like her sire Belin,) to the kin of men.
She goddess, leaning on her spear-staff, wakes
In this his loneness, in cold midnight grove,
Over the hero's sleep : and, in herself,
Quoth ; what is blind, brief, discourse of man's life,
But as a spark, out of eternal Night ;
That shines as gledeworm, in the world, a moment :
Or glairy path of snail, which in the sun,
Glisters an hour ; the next, of dew or rain,
Is molten.   Like to hart, of a great horn,
Fallen in some hunter's pit, lies here king Caradoc,
Man best beloved, mongst Britons, of all gods !
Yet is, of mortal wights, an old said saw ;
Is worth no weal, who may no woe endure.
    Sith, with her shield-brim, she traced round him,
        sleeping,
A circuit ; wherein enter, him to hurt,
Might sprite, nor wight, nor beast, nor element!
    In his dead slumber, dreams the glory of Britain,
He sees Hell's brazen kingdom open wide,
Land of the sunless dead, derne plain beneath,
Full all of dread inextricable paths ;

THE DAWN IN BRITAIN

Whereo'er, for light of day, hangs fiery mist.
There journey trains of spirits, whose cold graved joints
Lapped some in clay ; some lie in foundered ships,
Other cast under thorny brakes and moss ;
With creeping things, which suffer cold and wet :
He sees then glorious Thorolf go to land !
    But day-star risen, passed Belisama forth.
Then cometh soon up the tardy sun, above
These Winter woods, like targe of glistering brass ;
And grows glad morning light, from part to part.
Like to a pair of scales, thus chant pale druids,
In giant palm of world-sustaining god,
Is Day and Night.   What hour Day riseth forth,
Descends the baleful Night behind his back.

    Last stirs the sire, lo, stretcheth, in his sleep ;
For thrills the royal ear, ripe merry note,
Of throstle-cock, that pipes from thicket bush !
Like jolly plough-swain, fluting in his fist ;
Or who a-Maying goes by the green forest.
    He wakes, upon his elbow then upleans ;
And looketh him, lo, about, like one distraught !
Then heavy rose the king Caratacus ;
And in that seemed some staggering miller, pale ;
On whose courbe shoulder, weight is wont be laid,

Of his lord's grist, and who is old ; so hath
The warlord dredged night's hoary powdered frost.
    And yet is darkness, in the royal breast ;
When, lifted up his eyes, he new light sees !
Shrink now clear stars ; and come, the sacred Dawn
Is crownéd queen, in wide watch-hill of heaven.
Behold new day, unfolding, like a bud !
Sweet voice of early birds, sounds in the wood.
This snowy bosom of the mould, like mead,
In Spring-time, is, of gowans, blushing red ;
Kindled, yond hills shine, as some Summer heath !
Whence sun, like eagle, soars, on wings of gold ;
Shedding new gladsome ray, on dead night-world.
    Sprang, in that moment, mighty gentle hound,
With a deep throat, and licked the royal feet !
He bays, that rings again the Winter-forest.
And Caradoc knows the wolf-hound of the queen ;
Which wont to nourish her white hand ; and gift
Was of her father, Cantion Dumnoveros.
    And sees, in this, the sire, his mantle warm,
Girded on the hound's chine.   None other hand,
Than her own loving hand, him sends this token !
He it loost ; and on his shoulder casts anon :
Cold is his flesh.   Though climbs now Winter-sun,
This stern East wind blows piercing as a dart.

THE DAWN IN BRITAIN

Embla, when came not home loved Caradoc,
From king's mead-hall, sate in long confused thought;
Whilst ached her panting chest : to every sound,
Attent, her fearful ears !   When night's midwatch,
Past ; she sent servants, to Moelmabon's court.
  But those returned, with word, the sire went
      forth ;
Whence her, the more, misgives her wifely heart.
Yet sent the queen out other, in this night,
With brands ; commanding, seek by field and forest.
Those come to her, again, ere morning-break :
And found have they, how far they sought, right
      naught.
That raiment she then bound, on her hound's back.
So cried, Hie, Berroc! seek thy lord, seek forth.
  Returned, unto himself ; Caratacus
Beheld, like shining adder, on the ground,
That fatal glaive !   Him-seems, even now he Romans
Smote, or else dream were !   Smote he, slew he,
      Romans
Not, in great battle, this long night ? and put
Cohorts to flight ?   But, when he all him round,
The forest stems behewed beheld ; and knew
The place ; and all behackt that antique glaive
Of Brennus, which might well have holpen Britain !

For sorrow and shame of this disparagement,
(He, lord of armies, of twelve sceptered kings,)
Done to his royal state, he waxed nigh mad !
Caratacus, impelled then, of some god,
Embraced young forest pine, it, by the root,
Rent ; and he hid, in hollow, of swart mould,
Which opened had, like pit, his divine force,
The glaive, which should have vanquished again Rome.

Went up then Britons' lord, in his right mind ;
For he neath ash had slumbered, whose deep root,
In healing well, is wet.   Plumbs now the snow,
Before the sun, from cedars' lofty crest ;
Where gins to pipe the great cock-of-the-woods.
Rusht, sudden, an o'ergreat grey, gaunt, wolf, forth!
From craig, on Embla's faithful hound ; that towsed
King Caradoc's weed, to draw now his lord home.
They wallow and wind with hideous noise, anon ;
And grinning teeth, and long upstaring hairs ;
And, with fell claws, each other rend to blood,
Staining the forest snow.   Caradoc's high hand
A wild stone caught from ground ; he smote that
        brute's
Hard hairy chine, and all his pith was loost.
To warm his lukewarm blood, the sire forth goeth,

A sturdy pace, down from thick latticed wood.
He treads known path now, to his forest lodge ;
Neath brow, sequestered from the common foot.
It Moelmabon gave, to Embla and Caradoc ;
For loves Silures' sire, as his own sons,
Cunobelin's son.   He went by folded flocks ;
But bark the very curs on Caradoc !
So seemed he stranger wight.   His foot he hath
Stayed, yet unseen of men, within a grove :
For, lo, from other part, comes servants' train ;
Are men of his own household, which, (o'er all,
Having, in vain, him sought to-night !) turn home.

To Verulam warriors, message then, the queen
Would send, whose camps lie in the further forest ;
Calling them forth, to seek the royal footprint, ·
O'er hill-snow, of their king Caratacus.
Like unto new-born day, lo, weeping, Embla,
(Who die would, in his stead !) is now come forth,
At open gate, towards her returning servants ;
Tidings enquire, to read their doubtful looks !

Caradoc, yet nigh the sheep-pen, his lord, Gorran
Erst knew, lo, from yond thicket, coming on ;
And cast a joyful cry !   Then all, to meet him,
Outrun : before them all, runs Embla queen.

Them rime-god Caradoc seems, of Eryr's mount ;

(So dight he is, with leaves and hoary frost ;)
That, winter-long, in cave of steepling rocks,
Sleeps ! and (like chamfered fallow field,) is warped,
To ghastful looks, his wonted comeliness ;
For yet unconquered sorrow holds oppressed
His heart.   She kisseth him, with silent lips ;
And leads in, by the hand, (that icicle seems,
Closed, in her woman's feeble and warm flesh,)
To house : and hastes to bring, from sacred hearth,
Him posset drink, she had prepared to this.
    Embla new fever fears of his old wound ;
For yet, nor sense he seemed to have, of aught ;
(If he might smile, should seem to wake the dead !)
Nor mind of any.   Ran a little maid,
Dear fruit of both their loves ; that joys and plays.
    She climbed, unto her father's knees, anon ;
To Caradoc stretches her two gleeful hands,
The babe.   He her uptook, as one who dreams !
Looks in her eyes, plays with her sunbright locks ;
Eyes, like blue cockle, in the Summer corn :
And TAD ![1] the dear child cries.   She laughs, he loves.
Then, hundred sithes, he kissed her infant lips !
And were to shield this loved one little head,
Life, in world's mortal tumult, yet, (which is

[1] Father.

THE DAWN IN BRITAIN

Vast wailing place of vilain wights, wherein
Our efforts still frustrate the gods,) desires.
  That warhound couched, crept to his lady's feet,
Now bleeds ; (nor she was ware, for busy thought,)
From vein, fang opened of that felon wolf.
He his húrt licks ; gazing still on his lord, Caradoc,
Gapes ; and in that yields the true ferine breath.

  But, in the inner chamber, heavy sleeps,
All day, and the next night, Caratacus ;
And wakes in his mind's health.   Yet council druids ;
Till were the malign influence overpast,
Of certain stars, he no more issue forth.
  There visits him the royal fatherhood
Of Moelmabon, with his warlike sons :
And sent Silures' king, for famous bard,
Talaith ; who brother is to Mogunt, priest
Of the Sun's fane, of hanging stones : where learned
Talaith, (in dream,) to make and harp, of Belin !
Whom, when he hears, is Caradoc's heart refreshed.

  Loosed, in first moon of the returning year ;
Again, hath valorous Kowain ; whose swift keels
Passed, wind-borne forth by Durotriges' coast.
Night-time sith sailing on, by sound of Vectis,

In feeble moonshine, he espied new navy,
Of Rome, lie riding, under Belges' shore :
And being the most prows void of outshipped soldiers ;
Kowain some fires ; (cast, in their hollow boards,
Pots, full of flaming pitch :) other, wherein,
Were few fleet-rowers, in the blind night, 'scaped forth.

Thence, steering, under Cantion's brant white cliffs ;
They, in each haven and road, burn Roman ships.
But sith the wind increased ; and were they cast,
In weathers black and rough, out of their course ;
And, driven from land, still borne forth towards the
    North.

The third day, they make fair Brigantine haven,
Of Aban.   And, behold ! how at waves' brinks,
Parisii already assemble : who their dukes,
In war-carts ; the stout people, in a caterf.
For their sea-watch, which station on cliff-head,
Had, now an hour past, shouted o'er their fields ;
Sails seen !   Then, Are approaching pirate
    keels !

But when men mark, high-builded those war-prows,
Whose tackling and broad sails of Briton fashion ;
And, hang longs their high boards, Dumnonian
    shields ;
And valorous Kowain is, who them thence hails ;

THE DAWN IN BRITAIN

And Labraid, pilot of Duneda's navy :
They gladly shouting, bid that prince, descend,
With his : and all cry Welcome to their strand!
    Then every charioteer, some high-born guest,
Uptakes : who simple footman, leads forth rowers
Or warriors, to nigh mead-hall of Volisios,
In Petuaria ; of this Brigantine march,
Lord and high magistrate ; where then, eftsoons, all
Arrive.   And, after meat and mead, that lord
Hath promised aid ; when war renews king Caradoc,
Of hundred scythe-wheel battle-chariots :
And *curmi*, and bread he sends, to Kowain's ships.

    Parted from thence, returns victorious Kowain.
But come tenth eve ; when now, to Gulf of Severn,
They gin stand in, rose vehement wind : and borne,
Whither sun set, through long tempestuous night,
Are still, with weight of storm, their dark hulls forth,
Over swart billows.   Last, morn rising sheen,
They a fáir Land see before them, which is Erinn.
    And, lo, like vision of the blessed gods,
Is king Duneda standing, on that strand !
And people, of Summer-land, Dumnonians,
Known by their looks and weed, with the hoar sire.
    Who sailed with Kowain, see New Isca rise,

THE DAWN IN BRITAIN

On yond green hill : but might they not outship,
Though now the night wind laid, yet, for great
    billows.
Gainst ebb, men leap, from anchored prows, to land.
Then all go up, the royal hand to kiss,
Of sire Duneda ! and he embracing Kowain,
Praising his valiant deeds, him calls his son.
Much asks also Duneda, of Amathon ;
But chiefly of Caradoc, and of sire Moelmabon,
And Almain Thorolf, and divine Manannan :
And where, he enquires, is his son, royal Hælion ?
  Duneda, to New Isca, from sea-waves,
Leads Kowain, in steep path, then, by the hand ;
And seeded plots him shows, and his eared fields.
Follow, who came with Kowain, in the keels ;
But rue, in looking forth, their faithful hearts ;
To see, so strait their lord's house and New Isca !
Nothing like Isca burned, in Summer-land,
Of Foster Britain.   Sith, neath boughs of ash ;
Yet timbered no mead-hall, on the fresh grass,
Midst poplar grove, men sit at meat : they sit,
In long discourse ; till the new moon is seen,
With sickle-face, this third day old, in heaven.
  Then risen Duneda, father of his folk,
Lifted his hands cried loud, to the Night's god ;

That, like as he increased, might have this nation
Good chance ! When sith his shining wheel, in heaven,
Should wane, so might their griefs : lord, at the least,
Leave us in no worse case !   Yet, through short
    night,
All sit.   Few list the *curmi* and new sweet mead,
(Which Kamlan pours, in yewen cups, from keeve,[1])
To taste of Erinn.   Lords, in speech demiss,
Of Roman arms commune, and Camulodunum ;
Caer Isca lost, and Catuvelaunian Verulam.

   Quoth Kowain ; how should one, in Aesgar's room,
Deceased, be chosen chief druid, in Deheubarth.
And power therein was seen of Joseph's God :
For, in what place had Aesgar cast to kill
Those innocent strangers, on them, loost wild beasts ;
Was he himself beset, when he would pass,
Of angry swarms, from hundred hives, at once ;
That him, with infinite venimous stings, have pierced.
Aesgar, in fiery passion, grovelling fell :
And swelled so, that he might be known, uneath :
He gave the ghost, before the morrow's sun.

   But day-star risen, Duneda pours to Noden,
His cup: and sith, to strand, dismounts, with
    Kowain ;

[1] A. Sax. *cyfe*.

THE DAWN IN BRITAIN

And lords and warriors sailed in his strong ships.
Those climb aboard : whence, standing on their poops ;
They loudly all do Dumnonians' sire salute !
    Those anchors cast, in Severn gulf, that night.
But, sith, drawn up their keels, leads Kowain forth,
To go, by land, to Caradoc, his ship-folk.
They journeying, the third morrow, in long path ;
Meet with them some main-troop, of Roman horse ;
Which ridden that way, explorers, chanced to pass.
    At clarions' sound then, those, with levelled spears,
Ruin on Britons.   Shipmen, drawn glaives forth,
Do partly resist thus : part leapt, to rocks,
To trees, like birds ; fall, as from wait, on Romans.
They steeds, that pass, pierce ; riders pluck from horse.
    Gauls' brunt thus stayed, they compass them : on
        whom,
In disarray, Britons again give charge !
Rages their strife ; Amathon's victorious son ;
(Not less is he, to battle, on firm land,)
His foes discomfits.   When then few remain,
Those flying 'scape, by swiftness of their steeds.
Under his glaive, fell Virius, knight of Rome,
Their renowned captain, valiant of his hand.
And Kowain brought forth Virius' steed and arms,
A New Year's gift, for king Caratacus.

These days, yet more, in East part of Rome's
    Province,
Grows tumult.   East-men, on whom lately imposed
Aulus, for king, Cæsarian Prasutagos,
Risen, in revolt, rushed hardily from their fens,
The Roman *castra* o'erthrew, at Sitomagus.
    Trembles then Claudian colony, at Camulodunum,
Seen, round them, how blue subject nations rise ;
Though such be, only, weapons in their hands,
As hinds and ploughmen use ; slings, cattle-goads,
Bats, grasshooks, woodbills, bounden, on long staves :
For Geta took away their iron and bronze ;
But could not take away the Britons' hearts !
    Aulus, from strongholds and from towers, his
    soldiers
Withdraws, to march against Caratacus,
Who certain woods, he hears, holds in East Province.
The duke, before him, sends out troops of horse,
And expedite cohorts.   Whilst, by Meltraith fleets,
O'er wide salt plain, of ebb shore, those then pass ;
(New moon now is,) Noden them saw far-off ;
Unto whom, with father Lîr, mongst antique gods,
Was, of this Isle, the sea-waves' ward, assigned.
    Fared Noden pompous by, to yearly feast ;
Of blue sea-gods, in crystal halls, beneath

Isle, which then Sarnia hight.   In, towards the land,
He turns, with fury, his triple-teaméd chariot ;
And tumult great, of rushing wild-waves' spirits ;
That ride, as foaming steeds, sea-billows' croups.
And follow (an infinite spume-sprinkling train ;)
The, on gólden axe-tree, rolling, broad divine
Wheels, in wide salt sea-flood, of stormy god ;
And play him round, and do on him attend.
   Blowing then his sea-children, all, at his
Command, in whelky horns, grave note ! he leads,
Vast waters' wall, with plunging foot, on Romans !
Those taken, in angry surges, twixt sharp cliff,
And folding flood, in *turmæ* and cohorts, perish !
Ooze covered them, on that deceitful strand.

   The warsire, towards mid-Britons, lately marched.
He now, where no cart-way ; and cannot pass
Wheels of his chariot, rides on Roman horse.
One day, before the main of his caterfs,
Him chanced he went, by site, where enemies halted,
From march, mete camp, and foursquare *vallum* cast.
   Then was, by sudden fury of Virius' steed ;
Which breeze hath stung, and burst the rein, O
     gods !
Is Caradoc, in a moment, to Rome's port,

Carried. Foes swarm him round : durst none him
    wound,
All fearing him approach. Running, swift-foot,
Britons soon their sire raught ; they fence with shields :
But covering Camulus him, with his vast targe ;
Coursed his strange steed beside, anon, him ruled,
By the forelock ; and drew the hero forth !

Then war renewed, in Britain, as at erst.
Fires, on all beacon hills smoke ; flame, by night !
The legate marching, with assembled cohorts,
Them, each day, leads, in view of blue caterfs ;
But aye the more, with ensigns and with chariots,
Grows glast-stained host : come scythe-carts, from the
    North.
What hour, one eve, wont Romans halt, to lodge,
Rush suddenly forth blue Britons, from green wood,
With dreadful cries. Who first, thick spears,
    arrive ;
Fall on the legions' muniment. Saw blue Britons,
That fight neath wicker shields, then Romans' backs.
Fly cohorts, on whom Panic-fear hath seized.
Britons, with loud cries occupy their *castra* !
Blue warriors, songs to Andates, chant that night,
Of victory ; ánd they draw-off bloody harness,

THE DAWN IN BRITAIN

In broad moonshine, of their slain enemies.
In that field's midst, they heap then Roman arms.
  Come dawn, some Britons, climbed into tall
    trees,
No more perceive those Roman fugitive soldiers !
Who came, with staves and bills, cast these away ;
And choose them, of all Roman spoil, out arms.
Seven captive ensigns, Caradoc sends be borne,
On swift feet, through all marches of free Britons.

  But when Ostorius Scapula, Aulus hears,
(Whom Cæsar sends, new legate, into Britain,)
To Dubris is arrived, with fleet, and soldiers :
He in Verulam, (town which newly arms of Flavius
Reconquered,) now, disceding from his Province ;
In Galba's hand, lieutenant of Ostorius,
His late high charge deposed.　He sith to Gaul,
O'ersailed, returns, then private man, to Rome.
  And being Ostorius entered in his office ;
Though lateward now the year, when Roman cap-
    tains,
Were wont, to Winter-camps, withdraw their legions ;
This duke, into the field, recalls his soldiers.
He made recension, in the stative camps,
(Where those come to him,) nigh to Troynovant,

THE DAWN IN BRITAIN

Of Roman arms ; then leads, past Thames, West
     forth ;
Horse, new light-armed, with train and fourteen
     cohorts.
  Warned by hill fires, caterfs, which late dispersed,
Tumultuously return.   Behold, in field ;
As two night-stealing sullen beasts of forest,
Whose prey is murdered blood, that chance to meet,
In some strait place : anon, with hellish heart,
And staring hairs, and roaring open throat,
And eyes aflame, the other each defies,
Eager to rend his adversary's corse ;
So in night-watch, now cohorts and caterfs ;
Approaching, one to other, in vast wood.
  Lo, rising up the moon, in Romans' faces,
Britons' long, fearful, barbare shadows casts !
Seem flickering stars dance, iron light of arms,
Omen of victory, on whose thicket spears.
  Archers of Andred shoot, from Britons' part.
Their shafts pierce Romans' plate : who, sudden yells,
Thrown up into the skies, of ambushed enemies ;
And blowing bloody noise of Britons' trumps,
(That from steep clouds, rebellow in murk forest !)
Sustain uneath.   Lifting the huntress goddess,
Her crystal shield, surviews strange Romans' deaths !

THE DAWN IN BRITAIN

Icenians, which in Caradoc's forward, march,
Like rushing steers, then hurl forth.   ANTETHRIGUS !
They furious shout.   Who foremost, to hand-strokes,
Be come ; when, ah, gins heaven's night-queen,
    (eclipst !)
Withdraw, her light.   Withholds religion then,
On both parts, fierce strong hands, of warlike men.
Romans recoil ; but when, nigh dawn, Ostorius,
Kindling green boughs and holm, and raised wide
    smoke ;
(Which blows the night wind forth, towards Britons'
    faces,)
Issues, as from pursuit, by other paths.
    Caterfs new marching, with Caratacus,
Grown to great host, the third day, impetuous make
Assault on Romans, weary with long march ;
In cumbered ground.   Their yells, mongst thicket
    rocks,
Which sound ; did seem proceed, from neath the earth.
Their onset hardly endured Ostorius' trains,
Till eve ; then cast a *vallum*, in their midst,
In little space, and that behind their backs ;
They, night-time, without fire or water, pass.
    But come the morrow, Ostorius leads without
Their *castrum* ; and enranged, in haste, his soldiers.

THE DAWN IN BRITAIN

Blaming their yester's faintness, he gave sign !
And they ashamed, with shout, rush forth ; and cast
Thick javelins ! and with glaives and their shields'
    pikes,
To-day, rebut the barbare arms of Britons.
  Riding, mongst his caterfs, on Virius' horse,
Behold Caratacus ; who, hark ! with great voice,
His blue youth comforts, to renew the fight.
Esteem each one of weapons, which he
    bears,
As the arms those were of his saviour gods !

  The sire, sith mounted, in Brigantine chariot ;
Stands, like the radiant day's-god ! hurling darts.
But soldiers daze ; seen girded Roman harness,
Rome's short glaives in their hands, (like dyers'
    hands,
For woad,) on Britons' breasts.   Even Roman helms
Shine, whelmed on long-haired barbare polls of
    Britons !
Britons, with Romans, wrestle in the forest.
  Yet whilst this sun was young, came bands, by hap,
To that wold-side ; (where towers and, famous sith,
Shall cities rise !) of glittering Gaulish horse,
Whom Titus leads.   To-day had Titus cast,

In that green place, to graze his war-worn steeds :
Where, and the knights, his friends, would he, with
    bows,
Seek beasts forth, of the field and wood ; by brook,
And dew-steeped launds, and under cooling shade,
Of Summer boughs ; by thicks and hollow denes ;
And in the fern, whereas dun deer, lie down,
By golden paths, at noon, in secret glades :
And make them lodges, under crooked arms
Of the broad oaks, of leafy boughs, at eve.
    But when, within, heard Titus battle-noise ;
His Gauls shout !   Shout again Ostorius' soldiers !
That made new effort, with great poise of cohorts,
Bear bloody aback blue Britons ; on whose necks,
And wide uneven face, squadrons of Titus
Now impetuous ride.   Vespasian's hardy son ;
By valour of his arms, and warlike might,
Of his proud steed, shaking his armed stout crest ;
With few, brake through, bold riders, men of his ;
Where, in a twilight glade, in battle-cart,
Behold ; that great king fights of all blue Britons !
What glory, and might he slay Caratacus,
Were his !   They fight ! but the blue long-haired
    sire,
In skill of arms, and his heroic force,

And manage of brave steeds, exceeds, as much,
All Romans, as all kings, in his high worth.
  Lightly, the Flavian blade, he bet aside ;
And with broad glaive, in half-disdainful wise,
Young Roman Titus smote, smote on the pan :
It shared his horse-tail crest; and had not been
His helm of proof, had cloven, to the chin,
That knight of Rome ; who stoops, to his steed's
    neck ;
As one dismayed. Gauls, Roman knights, made force,
Then, all, at once, assail Caratacus.
  But, in that point, arrive Brigantine war-carts ;
Those which Volisios guides ; on whose shrill axe-
    trees,
Which fray Gauls' steeds, stand men, that hurl forth
    hand-stones,
And thonged spears ! Leapt down then, with immane
    cries,
Those hale ; and slay, on ground, their enemies!
  As drave king Caradoc forth, he calls to Britons,
Disperse them, by thick coverts and rough brakes :
So leaves he a barren victory, to Rome's legions !

  Verges the year : yet greater tumult grows,
Mongst subject peoples of the Roman Province.

5—M   177

THE DAWN IN BRITAIN

And when are floods erst bridged, of stony frost ;
Careless of fords and Aulus' towers, men pass,
From Roman pale, to go to free West Britons.
    But prodigies have made cold the people's hearts ;
For heard divine trump was, in Eryr, sound ;
And, mongst the nations, bloody dew was seen ;
And druids heard living groans, from dead kings'
    mounds !
Saw portents Romans also on their part.
At Troynovant, (that is now Augusta named,)
Smote lightning flame, the eagle of a legion.
    The sixth year running now of Roman war ;
When come is Winter, journeys the warsire,
From Caerwent, unto kings of far North March :
And Caradoc lies each night, in some lord's court.
    He lights, come to Cornavian Pennocrucion,[1]
From journey ; and sups in Ruan's stone-walled
    hall.
Was there, in Caradoc's sleep, an impious crept,
To slay him. But upsprung, from the sire's feet,
A noble warhound ; that the felon, pluckt
Down, on the floor ; now strangles, with deep
    throat.
    Upleapt king's champions, in the doubtful night :

[1] Now Penkridge.

THE DAWN IN BRITAIN

Those grope, in shimmering twilight, to the walls ;
Where, at beds' heads, they left, uphanged, their arms.
Hurt, in blind tumult, ere might fire be blown,
Was many an one.   His fellow, each misdeems,
That it was he bewrays Caratacus!

Light blown of dying embers, in their hearth ;
Men rid that wretch, from under raging hound.
(Half-dead for fear,) it is a cripple-thrall ;
Wont *curmi* bear, in his lord's hall, and mead.
Gorran, whose hand arrest on him erst laid,
Shows, this, lo, upholding ! long skean of sharp
    bronze.

Threatened with extreme torment of the flame,
That wretch beknew his guilt : suborned with gold,
Him servant of Cæsarian Cogidubnos ;
Who lately, a feigned bard, came into these parts ;
And that with privity óf great duke Ostorius!
So Romans wont, in their ignoble mood :
Witness thou bleeding ghost of Viriathus ;
And thou, great Roman, wronged Sertorius ;
Jugurtha, and many more ; and Gaulish Commius.

Ere had that caitif shed, in the king's drink,
Venim ; which fell Lucusta's hand prepared,
By the perfumer's art, damned hag in Rome :
(But feeling, in his wayfare, his old ill

Revive ; the sire would taste, that night, no mead.)
    And this, next day, was certainly known, by servant,
One given to ale ; which snatcht, from hand, the cup ;
Thereto resisting, of that wicked thrall ;
Who bare, again, the royal mead ; and did
Drink-out, to shining bottom of the bowl :
Whence being overcome, from the king's hall,
Men drave him forth.   The wretch went home, to sleep :
But so incontinently wrung him his bowels,
He left not crying-out, in his pangs, till dawn ;
When ceased his breath !   Came knocking, heard that
        noise ;
And gropes in, from the porch, another thrall,
For is this blind.   And fiercely, If any, enquires,
Do wrong to Ruan, or his sacred guests ?
But when he understood the cause, had license,
With wounds he slew, on wounds, of his own knife,
That fellow thrall ! and drawn his carrion forth,
On the laystall, to crows, it cast, and kites.
Princes and champions, with Caratacus,
Then sware an oath ; at king's bed-head, henceforth,
To wake, in arms ; and that by nightly course.
    Lifted, on immense wings, flew Rumour forth,
From Penkridge craigs ; and, at all Winter-hearths,
Uncertain tiding whispers, dread.   But Caradoc,

THE DAWN IN BRITAIN

Being come again to Caerwent, to Moelmabon ;
Is word, by messengers, brought, were burned in
     Severn,
And broken, at the shore, Duneda's ships !
And cause, few ravisht brands of herdman's fire ;
That empty keels, (which dasht together, ere,
And hurled to land,) in tempest of night wind,
Kindled.   But lords feel strangling in their throats ;
Astonishment ! that do hear, their breathless hearts.

When field's wide bosom clothed again is seen,
With the new blade ; and full of budded green
The woods ; and ere more leisure have blue Britons,
To gather, with new frenzy in their hearts,
Ostorius draws forth, from their Winter-camps,
The armies of Rome's Province, twenty cohorts.
Nathless, in secret of thick woods, to place
Called the Three Oaks, assemble East-men Britons :
And they there choose, in room of Hiradoc,
(Who, sick, lies at East cliffs,) and Madron hurt ;
Young Cathigern, to be duke of blue caterfs.
Mongst those glast-stained, is Cathigern as a Roman ;
Prudent and stedfast, to observe his season.
But when his war-youth, offered sacrifice,
Of sheep and oxen, eat their evening meat ;

THE DAWN IN BRITAIN

(Wherein, of druids, were happy omens seen,
Of victory ;) and would they straight hurl forth on
    Romans ;
Them Cathigern promiseth, on the morrow, fight.

   Now of wide-springing dawn, dim twilight is.
When erst might know a man his brother's face ;
Order them Britons : who then oak-leaf crowned,
First leaping from thick wood, tumultuous spears,
Assail banks, (yester cast,) of legions' *castra*.
   But suddenly issuing, from all ports, at once,
With clamour, Roman soldiers ! their light armed
With the stout thousands of Icenian youth,
Contend ; sith heavy cohorts. The wide plain
Seems shrink, under their tread ; and shine with gleam
Of confused arms : it saw, from heaven, high gods,
As harvest field, which wallowed is of wind.
   Then sharded soldiers beat back naked Britons.
And must, for all then his heroic force,
Young Cathigern withdraw foot. Britons betake,
Being many slain, them backward to thick wood,
Headlong ; and find new breathing space. But when,
From his mid-course, dismounts sun's flame, East
    warriors
Fall out, on Romans, journeying to new camps :

THE DAWN IN BRITAIN

And who them smote before, Britons now slay,
In their long trains.   Who erewhile them pursued ;
Now, they pursuing, redden their blue hands ;
And stain this foster mould, with Roman blood.

Sith brought in Belges' scouts, new word, to Romans ;
How Britons are of flocking youth r'inforced :
The sun shines on their hundred barbare ensigns.
With bruit those come up of vast Winter shore ;
Which beaten is of long wave-brinks' infinite foot.
Commands Ostorius, dig then his camps' fosse,
With walls downright, deep twenty feet.   Are Britons
Hardy and adventurous, to assail night *castra*.
But blotted was, gainst eve, day's cheerful light ;
And from dark mouth of heaven, vast thunder roars :
Sharp hail, with lightnings, falls from grovelling
    clouds.
And wipe desire of battle, from all hearts,
Britons and Romans, now their angry gods :
These, under skins, those harbour in wet woods.
But Belges' spies, which were, at dawn, went forth,
Being come again, at mid of day, renounce,
How glast-stained Britons were of new disperst :
Whose beasts, by freshet flood, the night-time past,
(Thus confess wounded captives, whom they brought,

At the spear's point,) were borne away and lost.
That water wide is out, by field and forest !
  Romans, sent scouts before them, then marched
    forth ;
And way hold, through Mid-Britain, towards the
    North ;
Whence aid flowed erewhile to Caratacus :
And Romans having need of beasts and corn ;
Their foragers waste wide field round, and steads burn,
Of Britons which lurk fugitive in thick woods.
  Receives Ostorius secret embassage,
In this, from Cartismandua, imploring aid ;
Fearing her foes should fall, on her, at once :
The queen submit her promises, unto Cæsar !

  Out of the West, ascends Caratacus.
Men go before him, leaf-crowned to the gods.
The king the wilds of Ordovican nation,
Would fortify ; and live there free from Romans !
Shall Kynan follow him, with strong caterfs ;
With whom the warlike son of Moelmabon,
Marching with his ; and joined to them is Kowain.
  Which known, through spies, Ostorius turns aside ;
To go unto West parts. Journey then legions
Forth, painfully, by waste hills ; and find no paths,

In coasts, where only salvage wights abode ;
Which know not grain, nor any use of bread ;
Whose most meat their ewes' milk ; and whose wont is,
To wake, all nights, abroad, to ward their folds,
From wolves.   Bear sharp stangs, hardened in the fire,
Those in their hands, for spears.   Great shock-haired
        curs,
Run with them : and from wait, like eagles' craigs,
Those salvage wights wont shoot down shafts, on
        soldiers ;
Which them *Cyclopes* call ; that find oft milk,
Great store, in their round-heaped, (like caves,) stone
        cotes.
    Last, when now legions, after travaillous march,
By squalid skrents of stony hills ; (where lost
They their most carriage have and steeds ; whose
        hooves,
Sock'd or unshod, so pathless and rough rocks,
Unapt to tread,) come to inhabited
More open ground ; the duke Ostorius hears,
Caratacus hath, with ensigns and caterfs,
And bands of oak-leaf crowned, (breathed in whose
        breasts,
Is fury of battle-god,) before arrived ;
And certain hold, now not far-off, besets :

THE DAWN IN BRITAIN

(Caer Caradoc named, in later age, the place ;
Where, in one marriage bed, of the fresh mead,
Bordered with flowering rush and golden flags,
And willow herb and peerless waterlilies,
Flow Colonnuwy and Tifidiog streams.)
This, building stones, repairs Caratacus ;
Part with felled trees, and heaped with hasty earth :
For will he here wait onset of the Romans !

   Blue warlike Britons, chanting battle-songs,
Sit ; and on whin-stones, whet broad glaives and spears.
Other new-tress long wicker shields, or stretch
O'er them new hammered hide ; some fret, at fires,
And supple sinewed bows, and twist new strings ;
Or fledge their quivers full of long war-shafts.
Then all their warlike breasts stain, with new woad.

   Approached, at morrow's eve, Rome's glittering
     legions ;
Now *castra* mete, from Caradoc, a large league :
And dying, in what hour they halt, the sun,
Seem the wide-kindled heavens as a vast pyre !

   Past is long twilight of short Summer night ;
When druids, in magic trance, behold their gods ;
That sit, on rainbow thrones, the skies above.
Belin, they heard, amongst those blessèd ones,
Far-seeing god, read Clothru and Ethne bind,

THE DAWN IN BRITAIN

Strife-fiends, abhorring his ambrosial light.
Consenting, gods then send forth, the night wind,
Which Grey is hight, from under cold North stars ;
That bitter rime, those hell-hags, sleeping, cast
Round ; and wall-up, in glassy tower of frost :
Yet, they ere day, through subtle fraud, 'scaped forth !
  Slumber caterfs ; but cannot sleep their dukes :
Strong are the enemies' gods ! wherefore their hearts,
Like rumbling water-mills, o'er rushing brooks,
Clap, in their breasts.   Kindled great beacon fires,
From hill to hill, when rose the Land-cry forth,
Make known already, unto farthest Britons,
Great battle-hazard of Caratacus !
That all make supplication, to their gods.

  Gainst this new sun, on flickering wings, upmounts
Blithe lark, from the low bent with heavenly throat ;
Whence creaking ghosts, from men's slain limbs, to-night,
    to-night,
Like gnats, shall rise.   Mead where the gentle hart
Was wont, from hurst to holt, to have his flight ;
And partridge cock, with ripe and merry note,
Now calls : when stills the dew, trode this fresh bent
Down, in long battle-strife, with jelly blood,
Shall, blackened mould, lie house of funerals ;

THE DAWN IN BRITAIN

A solitude, of rotten graves of warriors,
Henceforth !   Comes this new sun up, with still heat,
And shoots slant beams, like lances, to dull earth.
  Behold, the legate's purple is displayed,
On his prætorian tent, in legions' *castra* ;
Dread sign of battle !   Strait, he leads, with trumps,
Without all ports, his legions ; and instructs,
In field, vast shining threefold battle-ordinance.
  Beckoning their præfects, all dight arms, at once !
And infinite breastplates cast large brazen gleam,
As river were ; and glance, like blades of grass,
Their glaives ; and seemed, like leaping flames, their
    spears.
  Behold, then, Britons' bulwark, black with shields !
Wherein shine groves of spears, like lamping bronze.
Ostorius, lo, with tribunes of his legions,
Rides now, spy-out yond fastness of blue Britons ;
And their defences view.   Them steeps enclose ;
Part stony walls ; trees, banked with sods, the rest.
Quick stream, before them, runs ; uncertain fords.
  Returned, again, with speed ; loud Cæsar's legate,
From legion, unto legion, to his soldiers,
Spake ;   How those were the oft o'erthrown
    blue Britons,
Uplandish wights, unapt to handle arms ;

THE DAWN IN BRITAIN

Having no certain bond; and none defence,
Of helm or harness: mong whom to-day seen,
Few men, of war! Consumed, already, O
    cohorts,
Their foremost ones, have your victorious
    glaives!
  All shout to battle! Might uneath centurions
Hold back tumultuous maniples of their ensigns.
When known, eftsoon, their scouts have founden
    fords,
Sound clarions! leads Ostorius on the legions.

  From druids' altars, whereon burn fat ribs
Of sacrificéd beves, reeks pleasant breath,
Aloft to nostrils of long-living gods!
On craig stone, stands great-voiced Caratacus,
His people's Ward, amidst their blue caterfs;
That the walled border man of this hill-strength.
And cries the sire; Have every man, in mind,
His father's mound; that take not grief their
    spirits,
When tidings come to them, under the earth.
Better, in field, were warrior to fall slain,
Still turning towards the foe his threatful
    face;

Than 'scaped from fight, be on his weapon
    seen,
None enemy gore; nor wound in his blue
    flesh.
Better thus fall, than tarry long for death;
Till creeping age have so deflowered a man,
That he become a mockery, unto each wight!
  Britons, their warlord's voice receive, with shout!
Bright harnessed, he them seems descended god:
And, in well-tempered helm, like to a flame,
Of ceiled smith's work, is closed his noble front;
And dreadful dragon seems his royal crest.
King Caradoc, girded with that golden belt,
Of Togodumnos; feels revive his force.

  Great bearded, and long hair-locked druid wight,
Lo, standing on their wall, hark, curseth Romans:
Then casts, whilst Britons their armed hands uphold,
To heaven, his javelin, towards approaching soldiers:
Devoting them, to gods, beneath, of death!

BOOK XX

ARGUMENT

Britons' camp. Druids signify that the people go not
without their wall, to fight. Some, which heard not the
druids' ban, leap down to battle. Then Britons issue, on all
parts. Caratacus proceeds himself, to the middest strife.
Whilst the sun upmounts, their gods favour the Britons; but
when high noon is past, prevail the mightier gods of Rome.

A slingstone stuns king Caradoc. His noblest champions
bear the warlord forth, from battle-press. Belisama incites
Camulus to save, with her, Caratacus. The foot of Publius,
the prætor's son, first stands upon the Britons' work. Ergund
falls; and now the hill-camp is full of Roman slaughter. Soldiers
kill even suppliants unarmed, and women, at smoking altars of
the druids. Ostorius commands, to spare the vanquished.

Kynan, Hælion and Maglos with Kowain, leading their
armed youth, ascend, to join them unto king Caratacus.
Ostorius suddenly assails them, in their march. Kowain,
Maglos and Hælion, valorously fighting, are slain. Kynan,
escaped by hap, buries the fallen lords and warriors of blue
Britons.

Caratacus was saved, with few, from Colonnuwy field, to an
hill-cave. Hiradoc, one of the lords with him, sends thence
a messenger to Venutios: but he, being deceived by certain
riders of Cartismandua, with whom he meets, returns, their
guide unto Caratacus. King Caratacus and his lords, part,
with false Calduc and his men; to go, as they supposed, unto
Venutios.

Those treacherously rise upon him and his peers, in their

sleep : they take them thus, and king Caratacus. A speaking
raven flies, with word from Cartismandua, to Calduc.   They
come to Isurium, tumult in the town. Some, who take arms,
for king Caradoc, are slain. Caratacus and his lords, are thrust,
as they were, bounden, into king Dunwallon's hall, where is
sitting Cartismandua, the queen. Vellocatus falsely accuses
king Caratacus. Cartismandua sends again the captive warsire forth, with guard and Vellocatus; who shall immediately
deliver him to the Romans. Tiding come, at morrow, to
Venutios, he pursues after Vellocatus.

Caratacus is delivered to Ostorius legate; who conveys
back the king of Britons, to Romans' stative camp on
Thames; where, not long after, queen Embla, also, is·led
in, captive. The legate sends Caratacus, to Dover port.

Caratacus and Embla come again ; (but captives, now,) to
sovereign Rome. Venutios meets with, and slays the horse-
folk of Vellocatus. Cartismandua sends Fagl, prince of air-
running spirits, to Ostorius, requiring aid. The Roman duke
marches to Isurium. Princes of neighbour tribes submit to
the Romans. Cartismandua is soon weary of the Roman
garrison. That queen's last miserable estate.

Caratacus and Embla, come unto Rome, are cast into the
Gemonium. Claudius Cæsar shows Caratacus to the Romans.
Caradoc and Embla are led forth, to their deaths.

BOOK XX

Caratacus beholds, of his caterfs,
The countenance; how not many old in war!
Much part were children; when, to Britain, Claudius
O'erpassed.   And cries the hero, with main voice;
For avarice, Romans, fight; we for our gods,
This foster soil, our cattle, our sacred hearths.
If we be vanquished, what shall rest to us,
In our own Land, but the ignominy of stripes;
And, captives, to be sold to servitude!
And ye, O wives, and shamefast maids, be
    thralls!
Of your chaste bodies, to luxurious Romans.
Help Gods! And, brothers, lifting now our
    hands,
Vow we all preys! He ceased, and groan blue
    Britons.
  Dire shrieks, of frantic women, smite men's
    ears!
Are ancient wives, bereaved of warlike sons;

And spouses whose long hairs loost to the wind,
Yet in young age, made widows, in these wars.
Their shrill cry is, for vengeance, to high gods!
They dance then, with joined hands, in furious
    choirs.
To magic chant, kindling all hearts! of druids.
Whereafter, caught brands, from the altar-hearths;
They, madding, mongst that glast-stained people
    ran!
   Druids, which yet gaze, on the panting bowels,
Of sacrifices, send then to king Caradoc,
Word, saying; So Britons go not from their
    walls,
To-day, the gods should this blue people
    save.
   Certain uplandish vaunting warlike warriors,
Demetans, heard not, on Britons' further part,
The druids' ban. Of them, leap down, anon,
The foremost; gainst who, enemies, on left wing,
Ascend, Batavians, from the forded stream;
And thousand, with vast clamour, glittering spears,
Approach! Then Publius, son of duke Ostorius,
(Who emulates, in proud arms, young worthy Titus;
That late repaired, with Aulus, is to Rome,)
Leading four cohorts, strenuous, lo, upmounts;

And, made strong effort, beats back those blue
    Britons ;
Whose trumps, above, sound hoarse and dreadful note !
  Defend, within their works, their glast-stained
    warriors,
The Britons' gods : snatch, (thick as buzzing flies,)
Their divine hands, the Romans' shot, aloft,
And turn aside ; or cause fall shortly spent.
But Britons' javelins, cast from higher ground,
As they come on, pierce many harnessed Romans.
  Not long then might Cunobelin's glorious son
Contain his glast-stained warriors. Shielded swarms,
Whom those strife-hags incite, leap from all walls.
This seen, proceeds, unto the middest strife,
Britons' strong arm, the sire Caratacus !
Like as, who walks in forest, falcon sees,
And now not sees, which chaceth an hare forth ;
(His glimpsing flight is midst thick boughs and oaks !)
So in battle, fares the warsire amongst his,
And Romans. Champions, that tall Cerix leads
On whom his father had imposed, to ward,
With his own life, and lives of his strong warriors,
King Caradoc's life, him fence, with hasty spears.
  New vigour then and pulse, in the strong limbs,
Infused their battle-gods, of the blue Britons.

THE DAWN IN BRITAIN

Yet once more, they, in view of both the armies,
Would give war-glory to king Caradoc!
With Serpiol, (Togodumnos' burning glaive,)
He, mongst them running, bloody breaches hews.
The people of Romulus hear, bove battle-noise,
Caradoc's great voice, heartening his woad-stained
    warriors!
  This hour, must forge, of Rome, eternal
    chains,
He cries; or else them loose, from off our
    necks.
And bound, with fatal holly-oak leaves, mark
Men, is the warsire's helm, to-day, to death!
War-girt, he rusheth, in strong battle-press.

Is fame, erst laid strong hands, Batavian aids;
Calling on Woden god, lord of the slain,
On Britons' bulwark; and gan it disrock:
But bare the immane spears of Briton gods,
Batavians back, with loss of half their men!
  More terrible grows then strife, under the wall.
Issue blue Britons, like to angry swarms
Of stinging flies: an infinite warlike din
Wide sounds, like rattling hail, on a king's hall.
Wade forth, in battle-press, the barbare ensigns.

THE DAWN IN BRITAIN

Fight bands of naked wattle-shielded Britons,
Gainst stedfast bronze-clad ranks of legionaries ;
That, having overcome the world before,
Would win even this cold soil of Utmost Britain !
  The seventh year now is running of this war,
Gainst might of Rome ; nor Britain yet subdued :
Such virtue found is, in her warlike sons.
Whereas, in Summers few, had Julius' arms
Vanquisht Main Gaul. Stalks, mongst them which
    contend,
Death, from hell-pit, uprisen, beneath the earth !
In each of his ten-thousand violent hands,
A dart. In skies, his face the mounting Sun,
Shrouds, and above this battle, seems to mourn.
Lie fallen, as wind-cast shocks, in harvest field,
Men's carcases ; whose new disbodied spirits
Flit, without memory of their former being ;
Seeking, in the wild airs, now starry paths :
And gods all valiant souls receive to rest !

  So long, o'er earth's low field, then as swift chariot
Of Belin, god, on burning axe-tree, mounts ;
Their crystal shields protending, cloud-girt gods,
Favour the Britons : but, past his mid-course,
Prevail, at length, the mightier gods of Rome !

THE DAWN IN BRITAIN

Like is long brazen wall, the soldiers' front,
Of dinted shields, and harness purple-dyed :
Like then to climbing wave, that falls in blood ;
Upon a bank of bleeding warriors !
Breath of their gods, a little yet upholds
The island powers, but no more shields from wounds.

Caradoc, warlord, to what part, most, he sees
The battle-travail sore, sends strength of spears ;
Or himself running, (since, in this March, were
Not paths for battle-carts,) the loose caterfs
Restores.   But gin incline the wounded ranks,
Now, on blue Britons' part, of warriors' breasts.

In that, he turned, recomfort a caterf ;
Came hastily humming sling – stone, which strong
    arm
Hurled, of Iberian, mongst the allies of Rome :
And, on the neck-bone, smote the shining flint,
Twixt hauberk and bright helm, Caratacus ;
Where, numbness of man's sense, makes, nigh to
    death,
The stroke ; and so continues a good space.

As poplar, whose roots freshet hath laid bare,
When seizes tempest on his soaring crest,
Ruins from cliff ; amongst his warriors, rushed ;
And lay full still, divine Caratacus !

Then those make, shield to shield, the warsire round,
Impenetrable breastwork of their lives.
    Blue Britons, when the warlord's cry no more,
Above the battle-tumult, they might hear,
More feebly fight.   A coldness dulls each sense.
    Doth Gorran off his lord's bright helm, at once,
That might the freshing air, upon him breathe.
Then softly, who noblest, on his flint-hard targe,
(Which dights thick rind of forest bull ; whereon,
Shines, thrice enfolded, dragon of his house,
Whose fell head tin, the body is scaly brass,
Of horrible aspect,) lift Caradoc.
And him, to shoulders heaving, they tread back ;
And bear the sire, twixt lane of knitted shields ;
And save, maugré thick strife, from battle-press,
Of Romans.   And, from skies, Rome's hostile gods,
Beholding, did applaud ; and W o r t h y, spake,
Were those, in barbare arms, to have been
        Romans !

    Lights Belisama, by strong bloody Camulus ;
Where this, with lowering looks, leans on his spear ;
Wherewith he wont, in field, to strew whole cohorts ;
And thus she him girds ; Where wast thou,
        violent god ?

THE DAWN IN BRITAIN

What sun great Trinobantine dune was
    taken,
Called by thy name? Belike sat'st drunke-
    lew thou,
In mortal's hall, on ale-bench, Camulus?
Where thou the goodman's team, strange
    guest, hadst eaten,
Three beves; and sith didst drink, as thy
    wont is,
A tun of mead. Or, with thy wife, hadst
    thou,
New woe? Smote thy pilled skull the
    Morrigu?
Or pluckt she; crying, Dotard Camulus!
Thy beard? since lost thy brawns their
    former force;
Which could not thine own uphanged silver
    face,
At Glevum, save! but soldiers, from the
    gate,
It reft. Seest not? or grown too blunt thy
    sense,
How Caradoc lies, beloved, of mortals, most,
In swoon; and that in danger to be slain?
As valorous wight is murdered in his sleep!

Cunobelin's son; who burned fat thighs, to
    us,
Of slaughtered beves. But, and thou help,
    strong god,
The hero save, a guerdon, Camulus;
Such, at mine hands, thy godhead shall
    receive,
As shalt thou not be able to recuse.
Hearken, will surely I give thee her, to-
    night;
Whom long-time, as great riches, thou hast
    sought;
Nelma, the flower of all my maiden-train.
   Nothing; (loud sudden spake the impetuous
    god ;
Whose voice like Winter-waves, on some vast shore!)
There is, on all wide plat of earth; and
    dost
Thou, fair wise goddess, only promise this;
How great and ne'er so hard, the peril
    were;
But Camulus will assay it bring to pass.
  Swear, Belisama, then, that greatest oath,
Which is, in heavenly seats, amongst high
    gods;

By these three: Earth, which Ocean-streams
   enfold,
And Heaven, above; and gulf of Hell be-
   neath.
Then she, her goddess-palms, gainst sun all-seeing,
Uplifting; and, to far-off Ocean, calling;
With her spear's heel, sith, smiting the green sod;
Sware, Gentle maiden Nelma, of the white
   hand,
Fair-bosomed, should be laid by Camulus;
And he that enterprise achieve, to-night.
   Though strong, quoth Camulus, both, among
   the gods,
And mortals, am I named·; yet wisdom much
The power of strength exceeds. That, thou
   wise, goddess!
I learned, what time I marched to the world's
   brinks;
Where poised on pillars are, of heavenly
   house,
The starry walls, which stoop in compass
   round;
Or else, immense, should ruin on the world!
   Being the wide bent of crystal firma-
   ment,

(Their proud immortal seats,) to aery spirits,
Assigned for their abode, it mine intent
Was shake; aye, and split that fastness of
    high gods,
To wreak me; sith my godhead had in-
    censed,
In stranger land, Italiot treacherous god,
One red-eyed Bacchus; that, with wine, be-
    trayed
Me; and that hour slain was Brennus in
    high Alps!
  But substance entered in me, of the ground,
Blood of the earth, which in that drossy cup;
A mortal swift disease outsent those gods;
Which, like to lean hag, me pursued, in
    march;
O'ertook, and suddenly, unwares, she wrung
    my bowels,
With her fell claws; so that, on my bronze
    targe,
That loud to heavens resounded, I fell down;
And issued from mine hands, these divine
    arms;
And rang my war-helm, on that utmost
    coast;

And leapt forth, shining, to vast brimming
    flood,
Which runs about the world: and hardly it
    Lîr,
Sending, at mine entreaty, some of his,
(Mine ancient friend,) recured, ere the year's
    end.
  Three days, then, I consuming smart en-
    dured;
And alway in dread, of some strange hostile
    god,
Be found disarmed. And thence I hardly
    was
Enlarged; when taken of me dreadful oath,
Had those sky-dwelling powers, that no
    more pass,
I should o'er the weaved waves, from Island
    Britain.
  Aye and even this day me threatened
    Roman gods;
Before whom I am still put to the worse;
Were I, in this field, found, me spoil of arms.
One froward as a girl, Bellona hight,
A bold-faced buskin'd goddess; she that
    wont,

On Roman part, withstand me face to face.
Calling me *Furcifer*, much as, in our speech,
Daffe, Gallows-bird, upon my baldric seized;
And backlong haled the scornful virgin
   crude!
Mongst mocking Roman gods: me, factious
   god,
Of barbare isle, she named, before them all!
Aye, and lifting spear, me menaced, trucu-
   lent,
Send, gelt-god, chained; like Briton hound,
   to Rome!
Where, shrieked she, should serve my huge
   godhead's force,
(Yoked, like the drudging mule,) to hurl
   their millstones!
Whereat, they all laughed loud; and me
   derided!
Thou, prithee, Belisama, rent her locks!
  Day cometh, quoth she, when we shall ven-
   geance take,
For their light parts. Thou Camulus, raise
   loud shout;
Shall turn away, of those strange gods, the
   looks;

Whiles I so shape the substance of a cloud;
That it some divine messenger seem from
    Rome,
Powdered, with hoary mist, in aery paths.
In that they stand then gazing, towards vast
    Alps,
We twain descend to field: cast thou back
    Romans,
Whilst I shall shield and save Caratacus.
  Nodded, in sign he did assent, the god.
Two steps he made ; a pine tree seemed the plume
Of Camulus' helm ! lights, from the reeling skies,
Like as leaps charioteer, from cart, to ground,
The battle-god, midst dust and strife of arms !
And horribly Camulus brayed ; that seemed the
    voice
Of new host of blue Britons, which arrive.
At that strange portent, failed the Romans' breath.
His spear bare back a legion, a good space !
  Like swallow swift, to field, the goddess stooped ;
And closed, with misty cloud congealed, a plot,
Round the hurt king ; wherein she forms, as rocks,
And oaks ; and semblant shaped of a green mount.
There, goddess bright, she hid Caratacus,
Beloved of men and gods, even hostile gods:

THE DAWN IN BRITAIN

And like as mother, o'er her babe ; whom bee
Did sting, is she his ward, till fall of night !

He, who bare eagle of the fourteenth legion,
(Which   Conqueress,   Claudius   named,   of Island
    Britain,)
Seeing victory tarry, though inclined the fight,
Launcht, from his hand, his ensign, with great force ;
And it o'erflew last bulwark of blue Britons !
Then flocking soldiers, lest an infamy have,
Their eagle lost, the legion ; with main shout,
Rush under shields.   And, erst, foot of stout Publius,
Mongst those assailing, stood on Britons' rock !
    Full eftsoon is, of slaughter, that hill-strength ;
Wherein, alone, rests Ergund, to defence,
Of wives and altars, with his Mona warriors.
(He obedient, to that oracle of pale druids,
Went not forth from walled hold, in field, to fight.)
Three troops are his ; which running now, gainst
    Romans ;
Hew with huge strokes, and deeds of hardihood,
Them bloody path.   Till last, midst mortal strife,
And burst his lance ; was Ergund's immense force,
O'erborne, in enemies' great in-thronging press !
    Fell Mona's valiant champions, round their prince.

But he, spear-smitten in the mouth ; sore hurt
Being his shield-arm, of stout centurion's glaive :
Through-shot his other shoulder, of sharp dart ;
His thigh then, of a javelin, gored ; and pierced,
Under the left pap, of a Gaulish shaft,
Fell dying, flat-long, forth on his helmed face,
Amidst the battle-slain, in bloody dust !
And issued, from his lips, the mighty ghost.
   Lodged   on   two - headed   hill   were   Caradoc's
     camps ;
And parted them, in twain, a thick pale-work :
But now that rather turned to Britons' scathe ;
Whereas they running, and pent, like frayed beasts,
Are slain in heaps. Henceforth, resistance weak,
Find soldiers : Romans presently arrive,
To turven altars, where, to-day, is cried,
Were offered Romans ! Whence, in vain, stretch
    druids
And unarmed forth, and wives, which refuge sought,
Thereat, their suppliant hands, to men and gods.
In their first fury, all slay crude Roman soldiers !
   Now enters Britons' bulwark, duke Ostorius,
On his white horse. He, lo, upholdeth glaive !
His clarions sound, then, Cease from fight ! The
    legate

Commands, to spare the vanquished; all which cast
Their shields and arms, of the cerulean Britons.
Thus were, in field and camp, twelve thousand saved ;
Field, full of fugitive routs now of blue Britons.

This hapless battle-sun, at length, is ended ;
Leaving Isle Britain thrall and prey, to Rome !
Whose funeral shroud wide skies seem, dipped in blood.
Fly, to much slaughter, ravens from hill-woods ;
And groaned, in their high rests, the foster-gods ;
That haste fling night down, from the heavenly towers.
Falls night's wide mourning raiment, on the ground ;
Nor any went to Camulus' bride-feast.
Or was, the god his arms, from battle-blood,
Washed ; or that field glassed crystal firmament ;
Or Britain's bloody Dawn, would show the gods !
All night, the heavens, waxed red, did seem to burn ;
Which seen of peoples, even to furthest Britain !
And sending gods, o'er-all, derne wailful sound,
Beneath the cresset-moon, like lamping brass,

THE DAWN IN BRITAIN

Was eachwhere, nightlong, fear of impious death ;
Falls new strange dread, on drowsy watching hearts !
  What clods, beside Tifidiog's stream, be these,
Cold as the dew, which seems dank stars to weep ;
Lie wallowed in their blood ?   When this day rose,
In mist, were beautiful young valiant warriors,
Britons, whose bed of death this trampled grass.
And who lie, full of wounds, in field, alive ;
Have none to succour them ; less happy, alas,
Than who already have breathed forth their spirits.
  Yet in that night, was saved, Caratacus,
So loved him gods ; which, yester, took all seeing,
And sense, from him, of Britons' extreme loss.

  Their hearts are troubled that in this, new host,
To the warlord, ascend, from Deheubarth ;
Whose dukes great Hammeraxe and noble Maglos,
Kowain and Hælion.   Weary those, at eve,
Now sit, about their watchfires, in a wood ;
Whose flickering leaves seem infinite tongues of dread,
That whisper round : these night-skies seem run blood !
  They marched, at day ; make forth all that long sun.
Men mark, then baleful ravens flee on-loft ;
Sith filthy flies them meet : token, ah, this,
Of bloody battle-mould, lies not far off !

THE DAWN IN BRITAIN

Levied, at morrow, his *castra* had duke Ostorius ;
And pitched again, from that place, a large league.
But, whilst he supped, with tribunes of his legions,
There fell a new thought, in his martial breast,
That second Britons' army ; of whose approach,
He hears, by spies, amidst their march, oppress.
He sallied then, next eve, with expedite cohorts.

The Britons' host are marching yet this night,
Heavy their limbs, to come to Caradoc.
They pass, as in a dream, by moonlight cliffs,
On either hand.   So make they weary speed,
Till morning star ; when word is cried, to halt.
Men stay them, on stiff spears : lean weary warriors,
Whiles dukes consult, to trees, lo, and sharp rocks !

From mouth to mouth, then tiding, mongst them
  ran ;
Even now, the va'ward met, with fugitives,
From Caradoc's host; which tell of battle
  lost!
Deems Maglos, those were fled, for craven hearts,
At the first brunt ; and more than sooth report :
Yet reads, till might the truth be known of this ;
And they should learn, where now Caratacus is ;
They, to some covert, draw them, of hill-woods :
Whereto accorded those four lords, they march ;

THE DAWN IN BRITAIN

Yet hardly, in this new journey, drawing breath;
So troubled be their hearts.   Then suddenly, ah, bray
Out, fearful! in cold gleaming of first dawn,
Above, behind, beyond them, Roman clarions!
Fall on them Rome's victorious harnessed soldiers.

Swift-foot, like war-hound, through the host, runs
    Maglos:
Runs Kowain, who, oft-times had, on waves' face,
O'ercame proud Romans.   Shouts great Hammeraxe,
Calling, like iron trump, on who most strenuous,
By name and lignage, Stand fast round their
    ensigns!
Stout Hælion sternly arrays his weary warriors.

Did, heartless quite, cry out those fugitives;
Whom a new death, by Roman glaives, o'ertakes.
Time fails then Britons' captains, take on harness:
But they on foot fall out, each with his champions;
To hew, with iron, their way, through hemming
    Romans.

Magnanimous, ah, but too unequal dures,
Not long, that strife of naked way-worn Britons;
Gainst heavy-armed and bronze-clad legionaries.

Erst generous Kowain leapt, mongst press of soldiers;
And seemed his glaive, a flail, which thresheth Romans.
But soldiers hurling, from an higher ground;

Their sharp darts, wound his men. Hand then was
    seen,
Of hostile god ; which the unfenced body pierced,
Of Kowain, from the backward, with sharp lance.
    Thrust through the lungs, the valiant Iscan prince,
Fell on his shield, and on his comely face.
He vomits gore, whilst the fast-gurgling blood
Wells, from the broken conduit of his life.
Yet, on his chin, upstayed his noble face,
His dying looks affray his enemies !
In the dim vision of his fainting thought ;
He Amathon, the old, sees, sees his widowed spouse,
And their sweet babe ! and them commends his heart,
To that high wonder-working Joseph's God !
And, anon, ruins, on his reeling sense,
Dark purple iron shadow of endless night !
    Slew Hælion battle-path forth, mongst strange
        soldiers,
Which stand before him ; wreaking his own death,
Venging his nation. But when Kowain slain,
He understood ; calling on dreadful gods,
Of the dead world, neath living mould, receive
His ghost ; he leapt, with shout ! mongst thicket press,
Of Roman spears : and, without fence of harness,
Was the hero slain, of many glaives, uneath.

THE DAWN IN BRITAIN

Nor fighting Maglos, on that further part,
Yet heard, fell the two dukes.   He, where he sees,
Some Roman captain, ride on a white horse ;
First made his vows, to Mars Cocidius ;
If he him grant that victory, which he asks ;
He, to his godhead, would burn hundred rams ;
He on him runs, and hurls, with so great force,
His shivering lance ; that passed the flying ash
Ostorius' targe, and bit beneath his harness !
That seeing, rushed forth the son of Moelmabon,
To slay him ; and recoil, like sheepy flock,
Before the herdsman's hound, gan Roman soldiers ;
From godlike Maglos' glittering homicide glaive ;
So amazed they were ! Hurls, with him, a small power.
  But might Cocidius, come his fatal hour,
Not Maglos save.   The hero, o'er a slain soldier,
Fell, stumbling on his targe, mongst dying Romans :
Returned then, soldiers pierce him in the chine.
Which seen, his young men cast away their lives.
They fall, as Autumn leaves, on Roman spears !
  King Kynan, early, (who, with new caterfs,
In Britons' rearward marched,) was, in this strife,
Severed, by thronging foes, from the blue host.
He climbed then, in that valley's steepy sides ;
Meaning fall forth, from sideward, on the Romans ;

Where namely he hears an abhorred Belges' voice ;
Which seemed-him mouth of felon Cogidubnos !
But come up to sharp craigs ; so, on them, drives
Thick mist ; that, eftsoon, their own feet they see not.
    Hanging, with hearts aflame, on the cliffs' brinks,
As birds ; those hear the battle-rage, beneath.
Groping, fell Kynan forth ; whose furious hands
Impatient are to fight, from an high-place.
He astonished lies, where craig-stone caught his fall !
    The gods' will was, that were not Britons' dukes
Together slain all, in one sun ; that not
Them violate should rávening beasts ; nor fret
Them beaks of filthy fowl, they ordained thus :
But that the kindly mould, which brought them forth,
Again, should, in her sacred womb, receive,
At Kynan's hand ; and to late age, his praise
Be sung, that made them pious funerals.

    Ceased was, when lifted, from their eyes, that mist,
All battle-tumult : Romans have passed forth.
Britons, not slain or captive, left alive,
Be fled.   Strewn, with blue corses, silent, lies,
And void, the slaughter-place : nor Hammeraxe
Tarries, as now, mongst Britons' battle-dead,
To read who fallen ; but hastes, with headlong heat.

THE DAWN IN BRITAIN

Like guileful serpent, full of rancorous hate,
With quivering deadly tongue, and swelling throat;
In shining mails, hies Kynan, by wild paths,
With weary champions: and from craig to cliff,
That king, like hunter, creeps; might he cut-off
Fell Cogidubnos, or abhorred Vigantios!

Great Hammeraxe went on his enemy's trace,
Till Westing sun; when gazing from hill-steep;
His angry eyes none enemy, even yet, far-off,
Descries.   Then Kynan, with grieved empty heart,
Returns and sapless knees, from vain pursuit.

Come lateward, to that corse-strewn battle-ground;
His Ordovices somewhile rest, and eat.
All then the moon await: that forest-trees
And cliffs, soars now above, with silver crest.

They seek then forth, ah, midst the slain caterfs;
And find, woeworth, that do, in comely feature,
(And though already were their corses spoiled,)
And godlike stature, even in sleep of death,
Exceed, the Briton kings, all their slain warriors!
Kynan them and his lords, with desolate hearts,
Take up; and bear forth, on long wicker shields.

Totter their steps, afflicted of the gods;
For wot their weary souls, is, of her dukes
The Land bereaved; and must, a prey, to Romans,

Fall shortly! They to place, neath lofty ash,
Bear. There, delve their bright glaives the mossy sod,
And those together open one wide grave ;
Wherein they Maglos, Hælion, Kowain laid.
  Sith, drawn, of pious Ordovican Britons,
In the moon's shadows, are all dead blue warriors ;
And laid, in fear and haste, on funeral rows :
And boughs, of swart-green pine, on them men strewed.
Whereafter Hammeraxe deems burn this grove,
Over the bodies ; for, mongst ling and trees,
They lie ; where deep mould, of fir-needles, is.
  Kynan smote spark, of flint, and kindles flame :
Then sends anon, with brands, an hundred men,
To fire the thickets round : wherein, wind-god,
(Who Vintios named, to whom men offer birds,)
Doth breathe. Vast bale-fire rose, devouring roars ;
Which seems incense the heavens, and scorch the stars :
And all consumes, to stones of the wild sod.
That burning quenched, at day, sith falling showers ;
Shall bring up herb, on those untimely bones !
  But thence king Kynan led his Ordovices,
(With whom few hurt ; which found they yet alive,
Fallen in nigh woods, and hidden fugitives,)
To forest; where, three days, his glast-stained warriors
Did rest, him mourning, round : thence they turn home.

But is not dead, in Colonnwy's field,
Loved of the gods, warsire Caratacus.
Come night, his mighty men, whom shields the goddess,
Stole him away, from danger of the Romans.
Him bear, by turns, six warriors forth, on targe ;
Through hills, through wood. Now was, of second
    morrow,
Springing the sacred dawn ; when, shielding Camulus,
And guiding Belisama, in pathless brakes,
They raught some cragged coast ; and there find cave,
In cliff ; whereas wont harbour salvage beasts.
Therein the warlord, come now to himself,
His Catuvelaunian champions do depose !
    Thence Hiradoc, duke, who, with the sire, scaped
    forth ;
Sends a strong runner, to the lord Venutios,
Far in the North ! requiring hasty aid.
In evil hour ! for met now, midst his path,
That messenger with queen Cartismandua's horse !
    The royal witch, consulting magic arts,
Had Calduc sent, light steward of her court,
(Who carnal knowledge, of her, from his youth
Up, hath.) With him ride three-score young men,
    champions,
Of the queen's guard ; unto whom, she gave, in charge,

Venutios' kindred seize, for hostages ;
Gainst time, when Caradoc should be taken alive !
But he, whom Hiradoc sent, suspecting naught,
Nor Calduc's falsehead ; heard his guileful tale,
(How were they come, forerunners, from Venutios ;)
Returns, their guide, to king Caratacus !
    They then, that put on, day and night ; arrive,
Soon, to those cliffs.   Sharp stony coast it is,
Whereon the stormy eagles wont to tower :
Under whose eaves, dim sullen hold, lo, cave,
Whereo'er his thorny arms weaves the wild brier ;
And garlands ivy-twine, and goat's-beard, hoary.
Therein, (for it is night,) none keeping watch,
So far from human foot, king Caradoc sleeps.
    Lo, Calduc's men, thereto, with stealing foot,
Approach.   These gazing-in, that hollow place,
(Whereas none lamp,) see full of shimmering light !
It Belisama caused cast the king's harness.
    Come dawn, they them, before the wakening king,
Present, as horse-folk ridden from lord Venutios.
Misdeems naught Caradoc, who none conscience hath
Of ill desert.   He Gorran bade such messes
Set forth, as might afford that desert place ;
Singed corn, wild honey, and trouts of the clear brook ;
Bake venison, which ran yester in green forest ;

(Where Idhig's battle-lance it pierced;) that might,
Venutios' tired march-riders break their fasts.

   Now, by her aery intelligences, knows,
Fell Cartismandua all her steward's hap;
And Caradoc sees she, in a bowl of water;
Moreo'er sees journey, in far West March, queen
    Embla,
Folding her gentle hands, to saviour gods;
And turning aye, to heaven, her tearworn face.
   What heart but hers, had, on the queen's pale looks,
Not rued. But rues, nor pities, more than Death
The corse; or wolf the fold, that Northern queen.
Envying chaste life of bounteous womanhead,
She Embla's eyes joys bitter tears have wasted;
Which, like cold stars, for cause of Vellocatus,
Had looked, on her, reproach at Camulodunum;
(Of Vellocatus, whom, with wicked spells,
She sought subdue, to her unstayed desires.)
   Had Embla journeyed, from Caerwent, with wains;
Bearing, when Caradoc marched, forth, corn and
    stuff:
And way, among the wilds, now weary, holds,
Of Ordovican nation, in rough paths.
Another band Isurium's queen outsends,

With forged words, Embla's heavy heart to tempt.
Feigning the warlord, ('scaped by flight from death ;)
Raught to Isurium, to her royal court.

  With Calduc, Caradoc sire, ere midday, parts ;
Riding the king and his, on the queen's steeds :
(They unwitting; which suppose, to lord Venutios,
They went !) Are Hiradoc, Idhig and Volisios,
And Cathigern, with the king ; and certain warriors.
  By uplands, Calduc leads them, moors and woods.
But where they come first to Brigantine fords ;
Now, after supper, when, as amongst friends,
The hero sleeps, (and most of his have wounds,)
To them, misdeeming no such thing, creeps Calduc,
And his fell crew. On every sleeper, then,
Of the king's peers and valorous warriors,
Four champions suddenly seize ! Even thus, uneath,
They take the least. And though surprised, in
    trance;
With shout ! appalling all their craven hearts ;
Like to ureox, upleapt the warsire Caradoc :
And, with a stool, the hero had slain them all ;
Were not a wrestler stolen behind his back ;
Who, with a sudden cast of his vile foot,
Under knee-bow, where is the strongest weak,

THE DAWN IN BRITAIN

O'erthrew Caratacus, Strong-arm of Britain ;
And flung a noose the felon, on his neck !
  All, knit together their ignoble force,
Him bind then on the ground.   Yet hardly gyved,
With bronze, to this, prepared, they his dread hands ;
Who bellows, as an heifer, in his bonds !
Then they, that now his peers and mighty ones,
Have bound, do fetters on his royal feet.
  Those thrust them, mocking, sith, in covered carts,
And convoy closely forth, through much murk forest;
That might none hear, that main voice, of king
    Caradoc.
  Another day, come down to Abus[1] strand,
In moorish dale, twixt holts, swart streaming wide,
Rolling dark treasons, Calduc's impious breast ;
He weighs, (which all occasions should cut-off,)
Whether not Caradoc drench, and all his peers,
As misadventure were, midst the dark flood,
In that they pass ; yet dreads that river's god.
  Whilst thus he reasons, came, from the witch queen,
A raven, which she feeds with quicken berries;
(And, fame is, flesh of men !)   That war-fowl knows
Calduc ; when crakes the slaughter-bird to him,
See, and thou bring king Caradoc safely on ;

[1] The Humber R.

To enter, such an eve, in Caer Isurium,
When high feast is of great Brigantios, god.
It shall be light, persuade men full of mead,
He is run mad; wherefore ye brought him
    bound!
  Sets the sixth sun; when they walled dune Isurium,
Approach; whence blown, is to their listful ears,
As confuse noise of revelry and loud voice;
Praising the god, a thousand drunken throats:
Where come; the dune, lo, full of reeling wights;
With whom, is the queen's guard, dancing in
    harness.
  But when men Calduc saw, within their gates,
Went up a cry, none wist from whence, To arms!
Then ran together, presently, a great press;
But Calduc, with his spear, the people smote.
Likewise do those with him, that cry, Give place;
For urgent is this business of the queen!
  Way entering in, to the dune's royal court,
Twixt two paled banks, winds.   Cunobal it devised,
Is fame, for his more safety, in his days.
This privily hath now beset false Vellocatus.
Yet when main voice was of Caratacus,
Yelling he is betrayed! heard in the street;
And, in those covered wains, voice of his warriors;

THE DAWN IN BRITAIN

Men, whose hearts hate the tyranny of the fell queen,
Have, running to their wicker bowers, caught arms.
  Assemble, in the street, then, shielded band;
Which presently entered, following with the wains;
Shut-to the gates, behind them, Vellocatus!
  From the two banks, then fly his treacherous
    shafts!
On Cunobal's pent armed warriors; which fall pierced.
Bellows, within the cart, king Caradoc!
Who reads now all the falsehead of this queen.
The wains are halted, at the mead-hall porch!
  Is this, night's chilling air; it is no dream!
Those groans, in twilight, are of wounded men.
Hark, battle-yells! Lo, gyved Caratacus,
The godlike hero is, from a covered cart,
Haled forth of vilain wights! They, impious, thrust
On the great warsire, chained, to the queen's hall.
The rest, with buffets, then, unseemly, enforce;
With murmur deep, gain-striving, to high-hall:
Who, lords of warlike peoples, had, alone,
With them, the power withstood of mighty Rome.

  Sits Cartismandua, in her great father's hall;
Pale is the harlot-queen. In Cunobal's stool,
She uneasy leans: bright bow bears her white hand.

THE DAWN IN BRITAIN

Her royal guard, all beautiful young men,
Stand backward ; looking forth, with ready spears.
  But her imperious eyelids, from the floor,
Durst she not lift : she might not yet sustain,
Thy godlike looks, bewrayed Caratacus !
He Britons' king, (the visage wan, o'ergrown,
With beard, is seen, of great Cunobelin's son ;)
Fierce-eyed beholds, from under thicket brows.
He bellows, heard that moan of dying men,
Without : shaking his chains, he waxed nigh mad !
He roars ; and seems to quake Cunobal's moot-hall,
Whilst cites dull ear of heaven, Caratacus !
  Comes eftsoons in, then lawless Vellocatus ;
Whom so abased have the queen's devilish drugs,
He bathes him with the witch, and sits perfumed,
Drinking, all days, sweet mead, in king's high hall ;
Or dissolute else, in sun-bower of the queen,
(Built on the walls, adorned with feather-work,
And hanged with so fine precious lawn ; might seem
That dew-dropt weft, which beards, when Harvest-moon
Wanes and fall the first leaves, the thorny glades.
And storied it had fingers, long and small,
Of Cerna and Erdila, of Belisama caught,
With needle-work ; bright maidens of the queen ;)
Devising how betray, even Britons' gods,

THE DAWN IN BRITAIN

To Romans.   Sped his bloody work, that prince,
In ivory settle, sate down, with the queen;
And hopes, with Cartismandua, to reign soon,
O'er all North March, with the strong aid of Rome!
   He calls, for drink! Ceased now all noise of strife,
Without; behold, the ancients of this town,
Come bending in.   But, in their secret, weep,
Old men, that call to mind great Cunobal;
Beholding, bound, betrayed in his high hall!
In ignominy of chains, this chosen of the gods;
Who duke of the resistance of blue Britons.
   To them, with violent and stern voice, bespake;
Yet, on that terrible visage, could not look,
Burdening great Caradoc, falsely, Vellocatus;
How he would have delivered, to Venutios,
The queen. She only him forestalled in this :
And he himself must fight in her defence,
Whose blood derives, from that high warlike god,
Whose feast, renowned in all their coasts, to-night,
Isurium's citizens keep.   His battle-wound,
Which bruised his brain, makes warlord Caradoc mad;
Whence now, from his obedience, all be loosed.
   Beckons high warsire Caradoc, he would speak :
But straightway is shouted down, of the queen's guard.
Ribalds, they mock godlike Caratacus!

THE DAWN IN BRITAIN

Outcrying then, all at once, He is mad, mad, mad!
Stern, rising, in high settle, Vellocatus;
Steal the elders forth, afraid of their own deaths.

   From thence, not twenty leagues, stands walled Caer
      Ebroc;[1]
Where keeps Venutios, now, his warlike court:
Whom fearing Vellocatus, lest he march,
To loose out of their hand Caratacus;
His fell thought whispers he, unto the queen!
Wherefore, so soon as they might hear, again,
The people's drunken stir still, in the street;
They Caradoc thrust, without or drink or meat,
Anew forth, chained, unto the night; and bound,
With him, his lords: and, in what covered carts,
They now arrived, again, men them, by force,
Shut in.   Shall Vellocatus them, with chariots,
And household armed, strong champions of the queen,
Convey forth, to the Romans' duke Ostorius!
   They part: cries after, the injurious queen,
Come forth, before her porch; See they mad
      Caradoc
Keep well; they keep him low and scant his
      diet;

[1] Now York.

THE DAWN IN BRITAIN

Lest, journeying, he break forth, to some
    excess!
In that she spake, slided the harlot's foot;
In dreary slime, spilth of men's murdered blood!
    That great voice of the king, as by the street,
They pass, covers hoarse voice of trumpet's throat;
That seems to blow the vigil of the god.
They, come without the gate, their impious voyage
Pursue forth, under stars, and without pause;
Hoping thus to outgo the king Venutios.
Day dawned; awhile, they rest. All that sun, sith,
Taking fresh beasts, whereso they find, by force,
Those speed, till eve; they journey, yet, that night.
    Last, almost spent, they win to mountain hold,
In march of the mid-Britons; whose bleak cliffs
Like some vast chamber, in moon's hoary light.
Strait is the gate, betwixt two justling rocks,
Whereas their beasts and wains may hardly pass;
A fastness of such strength, that might few warriors
Maintain it, gainst an army. Vellocatus,
Here now secure, will wait Rome's duke Ostorius;
Unto whom he sent, with utmost speed of horse.
    Now, in that night, (abhorred of men and gods!)
Wherein the witch-queen hath delivered bound,
Great Caradoc, unto felon Vellocatus;

Were many, in Cunobal's town, keeping the feast,
Of king Venutios' part. Were those, for late
They arrived, not slain. Then leapt some of them
    down,
From the dune wall ; which fleeing, by dim paths ;
Stint not their running, all night, on towards Ebroc.
    Lo, those, at hour, when gin the leafy woods,
To ring, with sweet consent of the small birds ;
Draw nigh some forest hold, whereas abide
Four brethren, woodwards ; which, gainst lawless wights,
That border keep, for king Venutios.
Heard the men's words, betwixt their panting breaths ;
(Those left, to rest,) twain of the brethren ran.
From nigh hill-brow, the land-cry raise, anon,
That other twain.   O'er wood, o'er field, speeds forth
Then tiding grave, to hamlets, village steads ;
And gather warriors soon to king Venutios !
    Ere noon, are those two brethren nighing fast,
Unto Caer Ebroc ! where already bands
Assemble armed.   Those halting now, from race ;
Where, mongst tall warriors, harnessed, stands Venutios ;
One of the brethren, that assays erst speak,
Reels, falls, for brast his valorous heart, a corse !
    The king bade crown him, that lies dead, with
    bough,

Ere he were cold, of sacred yew.   Heard then
His germain's tale ; lifting his royal palms,
He prays the Sun all-seeing, far-shooting god ;
With arrow of death, smite felon Vellocatus ;
And give, that might he save Caratacus !
　　Now issue first foot-bands, from Ebroc walls.
By way that to Isurium leads, those hold :
(Shall king Venutios follow on, ere eve ;
With all his horse, and speeding chariots.)
March Ebroc's host, with blowing trumps ; and grows,
From league to league.   Night - time, to them,
　　Venutios
Arrives.   But brought more certain word, at dawn,
Is, how, with wains, went forth king Vellocatus ;
(And bounden, in them, lies Caratacus !)
From Caer Isurium, with strong guard of horse.

　　Found their wheels' trace ; pursues stern king
　　　　Venutios
Fast after ; and he prays just battle-gods,
With burning heart, of vengeance as he rides.

　　Ridden on the spur, the Romans' duke, Ostorius,
Is reached now to that hold, with knights and horse :
And covenant there he makes, with Vellocatus,

THE DAWN IN BRITAIN

At all times, send an aid of Roman arms,
To maintain Cartismandua the queen's part;
Gainst her strong foes, (now many,) in wide
    North March:
And Briton Vellocatus, on his part,
Shall now deliver him Caratacus.
Joining right hands, it, by his nation's gods,
Whom he betrays, swears felon Vellocatus!

   Britons, their warlord yield, to Britain's foes;
Yield, to be done, to shameful death in Rome!
There to be made a spectacle, ah! of scorn,
Nay of pity, even to his cruel adversaries.
Hero divine, they yield Caratacus!

   Called Gaulish smith, one who rides mongst his horse,
Commands Ostorius; he offsmite the chains
Of king Caratacus. Forbid it gods,
Quoth he, of Rome, so noble foe were bound!
That Roman duke then taking, by the hand,
The hero; admires, longtime, his royal feature!
His tribunes also gaze, on that great Briton,
And captains! he who, in swift-teamed shrill chariot;
And girt with royal band of barbare gold,
Leading blue hosts, had seemed some hostile god!

   But when is come new dawn, leaving that place,
Ostorius; Caradoc, captive king of Britons,

Must, midst thick-spears ride, of Rome's Gaulish horse :
They, each night, after long swift journey, lodge,
For peril of the way, in fence of *vallum.*
Great is their charge, who bring Caratacus.
Ostorius, in his tent, him entertains.

    Last all, to legions' stative camp, arrive ;
(Is that now Noviomagus, dune by Thames.)
And sith, ere this moon's end, with guard and wains,
Led in, sad captive, lo, bright Embla queen ;
To adorn, with him, some cruel pomp in Rome !

    Her, journeying, horse which Cartismandua sent,
Had overtaken; and they, on her, did seize,
By fraud, and her sweet babe.   Then, that fell queen,
Far ways about, from king Venutios' ken,
Did send them, with strong guard of horse, to
      Romans.

    They few days dwell ; and sorry is duke Ostorius,
For their nigh deaths ; who pleasantly oft discourses,
In tongue of Latium, with these high-born Britons.
Then he commands, make ready, the ninth legion ;
King Caradoc to convey, his wife and brethren,
To Cantion port ; whereas they shall embark.

    Such power he sends ; lest even, in Roman Pro-
      vince,
Some leaf-crowned Britons tempt, despising death,

Rescue their king.   Behold is led king Caradoc,
Midst Roman soldiers ; on tall Gaulish horse.
  From Thames' green banks, and all along the path,
Each hour, to vale of Kent, fast-flocking Britons,
Hanging their heads, spread disarmed hands and weep.
Fair women beat their open breasts, down loost,
(Clear as the gleaner's sheaf,) their long hair-locks,
Like to ring-gold.   Is, all day, loud and great
Lament of those that see their warlord led,
Captive, in their own Land ! and Embla queen,
That daughter of dead Kentish Dumnoveros :
And their sweet babe, the Maid-of-Kent, they name.
  At Dubris, galley-ships, lo, with stepped masts,
To take them in, ride ready ; and merry wind
Blows fair.   Ha ! mock great Caradoc's captive case,
Even at his own white cliffs, of foster Britain,
That shall he see no more, Rome's legionaries ;
Whose majesty them confounds.   But generous
      Publius,
Who emulates that old continence of Romans !
(The prætor's son,) taking this king's right hand,
(Which multitude hath, untimely, of harnessed soldiers,
Sent down to hell,) walks with him to Kent strand,
Where he inships ; and down even to sea-billows.
Last bids, with manly cheer and voice, Farewell !

THE DAWN IN BRITAIN

The gods, cries he, of thee, most noble
    Briton,
Have cure! Him follows, with their daughter,
    Embla ;
(To whom, mild countenance show Italic soldiers.)
In other keel, his oath-fast brethren sail.
    They loost, at eve, to shun the pirate-navy ;
At day-dawn, touched Mainland. Through plain
    then journey,
Of Gaul, in much disease, in covered carts,
Those royal Britons : sith, vast Alps overpassed ;
They turn, (but captives now !) to hostile Rome.

    Venutios speeding, with his warlike scythe-carts,
Drew nigh, the fourth day, to that mountain hold ;
Where warded was betrayed Caratacus.
But they now all forlorn that strength behold !
Yet of poor wight, whom, under beechen shaw,
Larding few swine, they found, Venutios hears ;
Was Vellocatus, yester, parted forth ;
With horse and covered wains, and swift - teamed
    scythe-carts.
He led away, king Caradoc saw, mongst horse,
Of enemy strangers ; that him hemmed, with spears !
    Vain pursue after were, the Roman squadrons,

With weary steeds.   Then king Venutios rides,
At second morrow, on his enemy's trace.
When fade night stars, and gins new morn to break ;
Being ready now to halt, and graze their teams,
They espy some wavering steeds of Vellocatus ;
That browse, with bridles loost, in the fresh glades !
   Blindness of heart had cast, on those false Britons,
Avenging gods ; that wander they distraught,
Seeking widewhere, and cannot find their path :
Nor knoweth one, any more, his fellows' face
And voice.   Steep clouds them seem some frowning
     woods,
Blue holts wan waves ; fire seems the wavering wind,
Which, their distempered entrails thus consumes.
For victual spent and spoiled, they gnaw wild leaves ;
But, kex and dwale, the angry Briton gods
Give to their hands ; nor find they aught to drink,
Of that earth-mother's breast, which they betrayed !
(Had these been scattered, before Vellocatus ;
Who slew his own folk, yester, from iron chariot ;
When fell dire frenzy on him, from the gods !)
   Like heartless deer, dismayed, at thunder's sound,
They gaze on venging scythe-carts of Venutios !
That powdered, with long course, to them approach ;
Whose riders shine, with glaives drawn to their deaths.

Then extreme headlong fury, upon them, seized.
Dispersedly, on sharp iron and whirling bronze,
They rush of him, who most expert of dukes.
He, like to erne, which, on his quarry, stoops;
Now on them hurls, without regard, save this,
Them make, and Vellocatus, ravens' meat!
   Men diversely report, how eftsoons met;
That felon Vellocatus could not smite
His rightful lord, the king, whom he had wronged:
And how Venutios held his wrathful hand;
And would not slay a wretch, beside his mind;
To heaven, remitting his dread punishment!
Whereof bards, in their chants, strange things endite;
How of crude fiends, in guise of immane birds,
Being ravisht; and long buffeted in wild winds;
That prince was cast, in dim abysmal place;
Strewn, with their corses, which had gods offended;
That stings of serpents, fangs of ravening beasts,
And ravens' beaks send on them.   Fretted die
They, each day, till eve: but made, at dawn, alive;
Each soul new wakens, to new direful death.
   Ere noon, were all his people cast away;
Nor more was Vellocatus seen of eye.
Men vainly him sought, among those bloody corses.
Howbe are some, which say, 'scaped Vellocatus;

And lived with Cartismandua, in secret wonne ;
In luxury, until, when changed her woman's mind ;
She, instead of wont love-potion, in his drink,
Strewed venim privily ; whence he swelled and died.
Yet sith repenting, by tremendous spells,
She gods constrained to loose her love from death.

   With strength of foot, horse and shrill battle-
     chariots ;
Then marched, against Isurium, king Venutios ;
Whereof foreknowledge having the witch-queen,
By aery intelligences, which obey
To her enchantments, Fagl, she compelled,
Prince of air-running nation of false spirits ;
And sends, by welken paths, back, to Ostorius.
   Fagl, gone forth ; enters now Roman Verulam,
In form of Calduc.   Squadron, with him, rides,
Of scythe-carts, whose hot teams vent hellish breath ;
Nor might, save by 'scance-looking of their eyes,
From women's sons, be known those hollow fiends.
   To Rome's *prætorium*, they presumptuous hold ;
Where Fagl proffers tokens from the queen ;
Then terms of late-sealed covenant, he recites,
Requiring instant succour of Rome's legions ;
For marches all the North, against her raised !

Fagl, in porch, without the council-house,
Vaingloriously, with his, (his reasons said,)
Attends, then answer of the imperial legate.

  The occasion, deems Ostorius asketh haste ;
Is season fit to conquer all North Britain :
Wherefore, the same day, parted ; he takes horse,
At Troynovant ; sent letters on before,
To Camulodunum, and, (new burg on Yare,)
To Gariononum ; to make ready cohorts ;
Commanding, that those meet him, in the path.
  That royal witch, who skills black weathers raise,
And chain the wavering winds, sends other fiends ;
Which, baleful, borne, on eager rushing wings,
Wake magic tempest ; lightning splits the craigs :
Is filled then dusking air, with blasts of dread.
And met with other spirits, of hell-ground,
Those make earth's face to quake, and reel the woods ;
Whence cumbered is the march of king Venutios.
  Sith when that warlike king heard, how the legions
Approach ; he rose from sieging round Isurium :
(Wherein all dwellers fear the outrageous queen ;
That takes off, and for aught mistrust she hath,
Whomso she will, by venim, or night-murderers !)
  Venutios hastes hill-passage then beset,

THE DAWN IN BRITAIN

Hemmed with sharp craigs; and whereby, the third
    morrow,
He deems, must marching Roman legions pass.
And seemed his chariot-wheels, as burning brass,
With hovering ravens' wings, so fleetly he drives;
Who most, of noble warriors in the North,
Is skilled, in full career, wield rushing teams.
    Bands, with the king, ride, of Brigantine horse.
An armed backrider sits, on each steed's croup:
Are those, in fight, light-runners, with the scythe-carts.
Three-hundred follow, of the land's trimarch.
Run many chariots, with the king Venutios;
And powderous, flecked, with spume, come their teams'
    breasts.
Loud sound the stripes, of hundred crackling whips;
Of who tall lords, in them, to battle, ride.
Glister their rushing wheels, uprolling dust.
    But looking forth, at morrow, from steep craig;
Far-glancing arms, of Romans' expedite cohorts,
Venutios sees, already past the strait!
He must return then back, to his caterfs.
Last he his weary powers draws to hill-foot;
Where now they rest, come eve, in covert place.
    But when shines wide East threshold of day's god,
As a vast hearth; to battle impatient, blue

Brigantes hail this surging sun !   Venutios
Leads forth his chariots.   Seemed a whirlwind risen,
Then, like to storm-god, on the Summer plain.
Venutios foremost rides ; and soughs the wind,
About his blowing hairs ; that, like flame, girds
A bend of gold.   Romans, at crow of clarions,
Though taken unwares, (had marched the legions' trains
Before the sun,) halt, range them, do helms on,
Embrace their shields.   Their tribunes, at a run,
Lead up the rearward. Time fails, stand in ordinance;
Soldiers them gather round their stoutest ones.
Gauls' horse, in field, with knights of Rome, ride forth.
    Impetuous assault of swift iron scythe-carts ;
(Whence barbare yells affray Italic breasts !)
Reap round them living swathe.   Venutios leapt,
To grass, and chariot-riders, with him, made
Yet more red slaughter : for the king, in force,
Though old, is next to great Caratacus.
Drivers of iron scythe-carts, then draw off,
To breathe their sweated teams, for come his spears ;
Which footmen now, in wide half-moon, he leads;
(Was this old warlike wont of Cunobal,
His enemies to enclose.)   But went not forth,
To-day, Brigantine gods, mongst their blue warriors :
(Fear holds their hands, dread quells their divine breasts,

Of FORTUNE, god of Rome; that, in North March,
Arriving, threatens hurl them from their seats,
Aye and send them, exiles, forth!) whence shortly
    enforced,
The Britons' loosely ordained caterfs are seen !
Brigantine bands are, each from each, dispersed.
But, from an ambush, warriors, oak-leaf crowned,
Fell out, with so fierce brunt, they saved Venutios.

Come to Isurium soon, from field of fight,
Rome's duke, behold, Ostorius, with the legions !
Where Cartismandua, unworthy queen, now him,
With feast receives and honour, only due
To Britons' sire, betrayed Caratacus.
Princes of many lordships of North parts ;
Then, (lest their dunes were burned and wide fields
    wasted ;)
Come in, entreat of peace. The imperial legate
Will, (hostages imposed and yearly tribute,)
To Claudius some, the noblest of their sons,
Send ; to be fostered up, in sovereign Rome :
But unto Romans, comes not king Venutios !
   These things determined, and left foot and horse,
For garrison ; hastes to part again, Ostorius ;
Had tidings of new tumult in his Province.

THE DAWN IN BRITAIN

Chuchid is up, last son of Moelmabon :
(For valorous Cerix, prince, is dead, of late !
Whom all men favoured, hope of Deheubarth,
Of his sore, many, wounds ; which he received,
Warding the warsire hurt.)   From all West March,
Chuchid leads warlike youth ; that come uneath,
To man's estate and spousing days, have crowned
Their beardless heads, with leaves, to fight, to death !
    But Cartismandua soon, queen, Briton-born,
Waxed weary in her light mood, of Cæsar's soldiers ;
That up and down the street of Cunobal,
Chant insolent proverb, in lewd Latin tongue,
WOE TO THE VANQUISHED ! shamed, she daily hears,
Her royal maids ; and Briton wives undone.
    Forlorn of all men, Vellocatus dead,
She now forsaken is of her fathers' gods.
Bright Belisama, in whom she hopéd most,
Abhors her, which betrayed Caratacus.
Though seethe she many a night-cropt cankered root,
Her magic spells have lost their former force ;
Despise her perverse spirits now her behests.
The griesly night-hags of dread Morrigu's train,
Conspire, in their dark watch, to mock her rest ;
(Wherein she shrieks, and weeps for Vellocatus !)
By day, are they as clarions, in her ears,

Tongues that upbraid, which whisper dark suggest ;
To slay herself ! ere vengeance of the gods,
Her overtake.   She sees, before her, rise
The souls of all whom she hath done to death ;
That beckon her, to pains of Underworld !
   Then goddess, Kerriduen, in that march,
Of the Brigantine women, on her cast
Distemper foul : whence, full of loathsome sores,
Might she be known, bereaved her beauty, uneath.
And her luxurious loins are thrilled with ache.
   In vain, to Aermod, goddess, which hath charge
Of healing herbs ; and, daughter of the god
Of leeches, Etain, Cartismandua calls.
Like carcase longtime dead, is this queen's corse
Become a stink : and who her lovers were,
Her now abhor.   Great queen she, in North March,
Doth only therein live, that none ease hath ;
Which, (when her journey done,) each thrall-wife hath !
   Moreover, seeks felon Calduc her decay ;
Hoping, dead Cartismandua, or else undone ;
He should himself sit, in great Cunobal's room :
But Cartismandua, semblant made of feast ;
She taketh him off, by venim, in his meat,
So sharp, that burst his belly, or he deceased.
   Then fallen in hatred, of all men and gods ;

And had all in suspect, the damnéd queen,
Used cruelty extreme ; and daily did torment,
As many as she misweens conspire her death !
As one past hope, sought Cartismandua, at last,
Atonement of her much long-injured lord ;
With secret proffer, to revolt from Rome.
But might not more entreated be Venutios.
Alone, he grants, in grace of her great sire ;
Her body dead, to bury, and not expose.
    In vain, she mullen burns and sacred vervain ;
And, in the thick fumes, mutters mighty spells ;
Which wont to open doors were, of dark Hell,
And move dead world : she calls strong spirits be-
    neath !
Her maidens answer, only, to her crying ;
Havisia, and eye-bright Erdila and Goleudyth,
And Arianlys.   The people tell, in form
Then of swart hound, the royal hag outran ;
Banning the gods, whose anger her transmewed,
(Her, hairy hide now covers !) to beast's shape.
    She delves, in graves, with her inhuman claws :
She rends dead flesh ; and that by covert night.
And rotten hearts, of who her enemies were,
Plucks forth ! (her hand the most sent to their
    deaths !)

To make more devilish charms, then on green grass :
Whence burdens her the people's dreadful curse !

   Being come Caratacus, and Embla and peers,
With long disease, to gates of hostile Rome ;
When it is night, and no man in the ways ;
To the *Gemonium*, (prison named of sighs ;)
All brought, in covered carts, therein were cast :
Where hidden, in loathsome den, beneath the earth,
As in a tomb, from heaven's cheerful light ;
They await the ignominy of most cruel deaths !
By strangling, at base hands of vilain wights.
   Yet erst will Claudius show Caratacus ;
(King, which these nine years hath withstood his
     legions ;)
A public spectacle, in the Roman streets.
   Behold then, on set day, those royal Britons,
Sad, squalid, chained, are lifted, bleak of hew,
Up, from that dreadful lower prison-pit,
Of Servius Tullius ; (which, four-paces deep,
Is ceiled with stone, beneath the Roman street ;)
Into sun's blissful ray, to march, from weight
Of night, to death !   Behold Caratacus !
With pomp, (great barbare Island's king !) led forth ;
By the world's sovereign-City's thronged paved street ;

And through triumphal arc, decreed to Claudius ;
Whereon his fond new name BRITANNICUS, writ !
Behold, bronze images, gilt, on that arc's top,
Set up ; of Britons' trimarch, and scythed war-carts :
And, in the entablature, battle, graved, is seen,
Before paled walls of hill-set Camulodunum !
  Loud trumpets sound !   Much insolent concourse is
Descended, in Rome's ways, of mingled speech ;
(For flow the world's offscourings now by Rome,
Wherein are infinite slaves of many wars.)
Stand, on all foot-ways, Rome's proud citizens,
Ranged ; bove whom framed be scaffolds, in long
    rows ;
Where sit patricians, and Rome's senators ;
And ambassades, with purpled magistrates ;
Women look proudly on, from every porch ;
Stairs, pillared temples.   Other throng house-tops ;
Where great Britannic king Caratacus,
Their Sacred Way along, towards his death,
Shall pass.   He cometh, lo, chained, like salvage
    beast !
Afoot.   With him fares Embla ; and, twixt them both,
Their little daughter traces, Maid-of-Kent.
  His brethren peers, come after, in Rome-street.
As, on Jugurtha bound, all Romans gaze,

On thee ; (with ribald jests, they mock thy looks,)
Sword-of-the-gods, divine Caratacus !
   Great king Cunobelin's scythe-cart, then is seen ;
Wherein war-kings of Britain wont to ride.
It draw forth, teamed, six tall young noble Britons,
War-captives ! and winged dragon seemed the beam ;
With vermeil shining scales.   The bilge is full
Of dints ; yet seen distained with battle-blood !
The wheels seem running eagle's claws, of bronze.
And men those barbare brazen hooks behold,
Whereon, were wont be hanged, in every field,
The off-hewed polls, of chief slain ones of Romans !
   Was taken that royal cart, at Camulodunum ;
Wherein is reared now of Cunobelin,
Broad sun-bright targe ; and hauberk of Manannan.
The shrieking Briton axe-tree, of hard bronze,
Rumbles, not-washt, with scab of battle-dust,
And rotten gore, on, dread, through mighty Rome :
And thereon gazing, shrink the hearts of Romans ;
That fear again the antique Gauls of Brennus !
   Thereafter, four-wheel Briton wagons drawn
Are.   March tall young men, captives of the Isle,
Beside ; upholding barbare glittering ensigns.
Those wains pass forth, behanged with painted shields,
Of island peoples, vanquished in the wars.

Gleam war-horns, in the first, and long iron glaives :
Bound, in the next, lo, thraves of bronze-head spears.
Passeth forth godlike, pale, Caratacus,
(Whose only arm a nation's shelter was !)
Betrayed, not taken, in wars ; midst dog-faced press.
The Briton king, erect, magnanimous,
Vouchsafes not them behold. The stings have pierced,
Of ire, his noble breast ; proud sorrow slays.
On Embla's looks, long-time, all Romans gaze !
Though she, from prison-pit, come lean and wan ;
So fair a woman's face, is none in Rome.
Her tresst locks part are wounden, like to crown,
Upon her noble front ; part, backlong hang,
Like veil of gold.   She, sad-faced Britain's queen,
Hath a royal majesty, in her countenance !
Like snowdrop pale, (the innocent oppressed !)
Their maiden child, she leads on by the hand.
(These oft speak, twixt them both, in Briton tongue.)
That little daughter dreads swart looks of Romans ;
And cannot choose but weep, because these chains
The king, her father, bears : nor wots, (amaze
Her, so sore, all things ;) they wend to their deaths !
Those peers, that follow, of Caratacus,
(His brethren named,) seem harts, mongst wolves of
Romans.

THE DAWN IN BRITAIN

The cruel Romans murmur, whilst they pass ;
What joy were, see these enemies cast to
    beasts!
Great-statured Idhig seems them Father Mars,
His harness doffed ; such his great brawns and breast!
  One led, lo, of the royal war-cart steeds,
Which Caradoc fed, with the white barley ears ;
And Embla's white hand combed, in far-off Britain ;
His mane, long-drooping, stains yet warlike woad.
Is he the last of those which drew the chariot
And royal sons of great Cunobelin ;
With silver bit, and barded to the ground,
With gingling little chains : dight his breast harness,
With coral studs, and emailled scaly brass,
Fashioned like sheen spring-leaves and bright-hewed
    flowers.
Lace, of great pearls, hangs, on his neck, of glass.
  Not as when Hart-foot, with his dam, Blue-mane ;
Or his yoke-fellow, swift Gold-hoof, he ran,
Under bright silver yoke-tree of Cunobelin ;
And shook the hulver-beam of the king's chariot.
Wound-weary old, this famous battle-steed,
Gaul's long paved way, and, sith, vast Alps hath
    passed.
On his broad chine, hath carrion leanness seized.

THE DAWN IN BRITAIN

His bronze-shod hooves, which wont, in island Britain,
To trample Roman shields, uneath tread forth.
Of stature low, he goeth, in Rome's paved street,
With drooping crest.   And heard, mongst mocking
    Romans,
Was word, from mouth to mouth, Whether is this
The horse or ass, of king Caratacus?
   They gaze on arms upborne, of tall blue warriors,
On staves and tables, of two Briton kings.
But most Manannan's hauberk Rome admires ;
That casts, divine, a strange victorious gleam !
Much like quaint precious armure which uphangs,
In temple of Bellona, of Britomaros ;[1]
Or that of Gaulish king Bituitus ;[2]
Who rode in Fabius' triumph, of old time ;
In silver war-cart, clad in gilt ceiled harness.
   Men gaze on Caradoc's helm, of lucid steel,
Whose crest that dragon of his royal house ;
And golden belt of strength, and tremble Romans :
And the king's glaive, which heapmeal hath slain
    soldiers.
The same is noised, was sword renowned, that Brennus
Cast in those antique balances of old Rome !

[1] Duke of Senones, defeated B.C. 283.
[2] King of Arverni, defeated B.C. 121.

THE DAWN IN BRITAIN

Yet seen borne collars, kingly ornaments,
Gold frets, broad brooches, rings and long-spired
    bracelets,
Cups, silver mead-horns of old Verulam kings ;
Gold bends of charioteers, bright tyres of steeds ;
Then spoil of infinite bronze, lead, silver, tin.
Last princes, hostages, of submitted tribes,
Of Britons, march ; about whose noble necks,
Wreathed *torques* shine, of the fine burnt gold of
    Britain !

Printed by T. and A. CONSTABLE, Printers to His Majesty
at the Edinburgh University Press